MORE OF EVERYTHING

How I became a better parent to my child with extreme special needs by lifting my emotional burdens.

Published by Janie Reade LLC
1211 E Denny Way #B53, Seattle, WA 98122

Book Design by Gyoung Soon Choi
Cover Art by Rhianon Paige and Gyoung Soon Choi

To all who keep showing up, despite worry and sadness.

FOREWORD

Wherever you are on your parenting journey, More of Everything offers you more than you might expect. While reading Janie's descriptions of life with her son, Joey, born with "a complex and intense set of needs," I was simultaneously humbled and in awe. As a divorced, single mom of two rambunctious sons, 21 months apart, co-parenting with a father who struggled with mental illness, I learned some things about acceptance, patience and perseverance. I could relate to Janie's experiences—but only to a point. The extreme needs of her son, coupled with a medical system that couldn't provide a reasonable path forward, would push anyone to the brink. Yet, Janie deliberately, and with careful self-awareness, worked on her acceptance, patience, and perseverance, day by grueling day, strengthening each quality with every passing year. Consequently, More of Everything acts as an inspiring guide, not only for moms of special needs children, but for any parent going through complex experiences. And that means it is an inspiring guide for most of us!

The book also acts as a motivational model. For instance, usually if we don't experience something directly, it is difficult to imagine it. Yet, because of Janie's authentic sharing—candidly without any sugar-coating—the reader re-lives her ups and downs, failures and successes, along with the gamut of emotions that went with them. We are by her side every step of the way, wanting to catch her when she is falling, softly chide her when she is being hard on herself, and celebrate those small victories with her as she smiles through the tears. And in rooting for her, we can't help but be motivated to do the same for ourselves when faced with perplexing, frustrating challenges.

More of Everything is ultimately a primer on growth as a relational process. Each snippet about parenting Joey from birth through age 21, has us also observing Janie's growth as she works so hard to help Joey grow. Janie's background as a scientist made me think of the old adage that each of us is the best-fit parent for our child. If children do choose their parents, Joey couldn't have chosen a wiser, better Mom! Her relentless research and dogged determination to find the right therapists, doctors, and helpers, model for all of us how we can use our own knowledge and intuition to make the best decisions for our children. And because Janie willingly sacrificed her career, you can't help but think about what mothers give up to parent their children, and what they gain because of those decisions, as well. Our children become necessary partners in our own growth.

Janie was always conscious of this fact. She naturally has a "growth mind-set," constantly coming up with creative ideas for helping Joey as well as herself. She reached out to support networks and found life-long friends whom she could relate to who were going through similar experiences. She was continually open to new approaches and better ideas—willing to explore and try on whatever worked. And that led her to a coach who opened the door to greater self-understanding, bringing more peace and clarity into her life, and Joey's as well.

There are many valuable lessons in this poignant and profound book. The one that stands out for me, not written about here, but one that I infer from Janie's journey, is the lesson of the "wounded healer." Inspired by ancient Greek Mythology and developed by Carl Jung, the concept of the wounded healer describes healers as professionals who themselves suffered greatly and decide to use their hard-won wisdom to help others. Janie, as a PCI Certified Parent Coach®, brings a wealth of experience and understanding to her work. Actually, it's amazing --just like Joey picked the right Mom -- Janie picked the right next profession.

When you read More of Everything you will see what I mean.

Gloria DeGaetano
Founder/CEO, Parent Coaching Institute

CONTENTS

Introduction

I am the mother of a 21-year-old with extreme special needs. On the day after his first birthday, Joey was diagnosed with what were obvious developmental delays. I spent the first six years of his life determined to help him catch up, grappling with his stalled learning trajectory, his inability to sleep, and his dangerously high pain threshold. He was diagnosed with autism just before his fourth birthday. Joey did not develop many communication skills – speech, pointing or other gestures -- other than protesting by biting his own hand. He had trouble swallowing as well as food aversions and gut difficulties that required extraordinary measures to keep his weight in a healthy range. During the few times that I was able to hold him still enough to help a neurologist glue dozens of electrical leads to his scalp, we saw abnormal brain wave patterns.

After age six, Joey developed anxiety so severe that it interrupted his growth, and at 14 an X-ray of his hand revealed a four-year delay of his bone age. When he was 16, during his fifth round of genetic testing, we found the cause of his differences: Joey is missing one nucleotide from one copy of an essential gene. This collection of facts highlights how Joey is unlike his two brothers and everyone else I know.

Joey lives with a lifelong neurodevelopmental disorder caused by a mutation in the Syngap1 gene. As of 2022 there are about a thousand families worldwide that have joined the Syngap1 rare disease community. Scientists predict that hundreds of thousands more people currently live with this disorder but have not yet had genetic testing to identify the source of their intellectual disability, epilepsy, autism, and other challenges. My son's diagnosis is rare but our experience is not: mutations in at least 500 other genes also cause neurodevelopmental disorders.

Joey has medical issues. He has cognitive impairment. He has behaviors that are difficult for him and the people who care for him. Yes, he has special needs, but that phrase misrepresents the sum of his challenges. When I examine each way that he needs support, none is out of the ordinary, or special. Some of his needs are appropriate for a toddler, because that is his developmental stage. Some needs are more intense than you would expect, as his emotional regulation is neither consistent nor robust. Many of his needs are more difficult because he continues to grow stronger without learning to tolerate daily care routines. His medical needs are shared by many people without the label "special." He has a complex and intense set of needs that I would describe as extreme.

I am trained as a scientist. I completed a typical academic education: a four-year college degree followed by six years of graduate school followed by a five-year postdoctoral fellowship. I am fueled by curiosity. I experienced pure joy in the experimental and theoretical breakthroughs I was lucky enough to be part of. I came to motherhood as someone who naturally observes and analyzes. I also rely on my scientific mind to have faith that Joey's unusual behaviors make sense from his perspective, and to know that my job is to try to understand him. Research, trial and error, and finding a broad range of mentors are essential for me.

Now that Joey is a young adult, I find myself reflecting on our unusual mother-son relationship. Parenting him is still mystifying and thrilling, difficult and rewarding, surprising and basic. This small book follows my emotional journey while being Joey's mom. I deliberately leave out my husband's role in Joey's life and most of my role as the mom of my other kids. I focus on what I can control: my own insights and changes within me that impact my relationship with Joey. I hope that reading my book will help anyone who wants to look inside themselves to improve their relationship with their child. I am so sure of the efficient and transformational good that can come from this work that I've dedicated my professional life to parent coaching, helping others to feel better about their parenting and to be better parents.

Part One of this book contains a series of vignettes covering a range of issues I faced while parenting Joey. With each anecdote I've included a section called LOOKING BACK, which contains some related summary and analysis. In a section called MY TAKEAWAYS I offer a few conclusions and learned wisdom of my own.

Part Two covers the major journeys of acceptance and frustration that are common for families dealing with a severe neurodevelopmental diagnosis.

Part Three introduces Parent Coaching. Throughout this book, my goal is to be as honest as I can about my thoughts and feelings, and how they have changed over time.

Emotions: Age 4

more of everything

I stand still in my entryway at home. I clamp down my urge to run around and call out for my son. I strain to hear any sound: the drop of a toy, or Joey's soft steady breath. I'm searching for my princely 4-year-old, with a long nose, wide mouth, and impossibly soft skin. We were just in the kitchen, and I left the baby gate open. I set him down to wash the dishes and he walked away without me noticing.

Every parent feels urgency when looking for their missing toddler, but I'm in full panic. Joey could easily harm himself just about anywhere because he can barely feel pain. Despite unremitting therapies, Joey cannot speak or follow directions. I hold him for much of the day, coaxing him to engage in my world. Stay-at-home parenting was my choice even before Joey showed developmental delays. Our plan to have three kids quickly was a success, and I was excited to enjoy shepherding them all through early childhood bliss and get back to my science career.

After a moment of agonizing silence, I charge ahead. He is not by the toys in the front room, or about to fall down the stairs, or near the heavy fireplace tools. When I see him sitting quietly beyond the couch, my worry dissolves. I feel foolish for my inflated fear. Still, I chastise myself for letting him be at risk.

I have no idea how to teach Joey to recognize and avoid danger. I have support from family, friends, doctors, therapists, and teachers, but no one has made a difference in his abilities. No one understands my overwhelming drive to help him communicate and develop, while avoiding collateral damage to our other two kids.

I watch Joey sit perfectly still. His steady, blank stare questions why I have yet to pick him up. I want him to know he's not supposed to be in the living room alone, but how can I tell him so he'll understand? I've already tried everything. Repeatedly.

Frustration erupts out of me in a slow shaky movement. I point at the ceiling, then pivot my straight arm to reach for the doorway, while I hear my low trembling voice stretch the word "OUT," strange and unflattering. Despite (or perhaps because of) my clown-like aggravation, my face continues to hold his attention.

My beautiful boy lifts one arm to horizontal and manages something like "ooowww."

I cough a combined laugh and sob. This is the first time he's mimicked me. I rush to scoop him up. I hold him facing me, one forearm under his bottom, the other along his back; my hand supports his floppy neck and heavy head. I'm grinning at him and crying, twisting back and forth, with the cheerful agitation of a top-load washer. "Out! Yes! Out!"

Pride and joy crowd out my bewilderment, leaving laughter through tears.

It will be a long time before he mimics me again.

LOOKING BACK

I felt panic, guilt, relief, frustration, shame, pride, and unbridled joy, all in the space of about a minute. Under it all was a foundation of unwelcome sadness. I don't think that my range of emotions is wider because of my different child. I notice, though, that the highs and lows are closer together, and I experience unrelated, even opposite feelings at the same time.

Parenting Joey feels different than I expect.

It feels like more of everything.

MY TAKEAWAYS

1. It is normal for me to feel multiple intense emotions, all at once or close together.

2. It is normal for Joey to surprise me by doing something new and then not repeat it.

3. It is normal for me to feel sad nearly all the time, even while feeling positive emotions.

Therapies: age 5

maybe this will work

When Joey is five years old, I run into a friend I met at the Birth-to-Three Center during transition songs and calendar time. Her son is two years older than Joey, so I consider her a veteran at navigating this alternate lifestyle. She explains to me how she came to realize that more therapy sessions aren't better for her developmentally delayed child. "I was racing to our private Occupational Therapy session at 60 miles an hour. I started to nod off because I was so tired. That moment was it for me. It was so dangerous. I could have killed us both. I cancelled our weekly appointment so we could sleep in. I had to prioritize our wellbeing."

I admire her for her honesty and marvel that her priorities are so clear. I wonder what my anecdote will be -- the one I tell parents coming up behind me. It won't be the same one.

I've been researching for years already. I know about therapies for autism, treatments for brain-injured children, and exercises for the optimal development of neurotypical children. There aren't enough hours in the week to do it all. I make lists and phone calls, trying to find a schedule that includes something that might make a difference, might revive Joey's stalled development. He often sleeps only five or six hours a night, so skipping appointments won't get me more rest. The clock is running out on the "five- to six-year-old" range that his pediatricians and neurologists suggested for when to start worrying about his lack of speech.

It isn't just that Joey isn't talking. He isn't listening, or imitating, or initiating communication except with a grab when he wants me to do something, or a hit or a bite when he objects to what's going on. I leverage the things he likes (ice cream, swings, elevators) into rewards in exchange for something, anything from him. Sometimes he produces a word approximation or a hand gesture in an attempt at sign language. Depending on the equipment at hand, he also might touch a picture (Picture Exchange Communication System), use an augmentative communication device (Dynavox, Tango!, iPad), point to something I've drawn on a sketchbook, or indicate one of two choices offered. When it's not going well, I read his gaze, which follows what he wants, or I look for motion in his body, which is peacefully still unless he really tries to move.

Joey qualifies for many types of therapy, and we go. Physical Therapists try to teach him to ride a tricycle and sit on an exercise ball. Occupational Therapists try to teach him to put pegs in holes and pop bubbles. Speech Therapists try to teach him to move his mouth, speak, and understand words. The PT/OT/Speech triumvirate found in schools and private practice is only the beginning. I find a European-trained developmental specialist who uses a form of Listening Therapy and other sensory and movement activities to try to grow up his nervous system. I find horseback riding that wakes up his core muscles. Hippotherapy turns out to be the hour of each week when he is the most engaged with others, at least for the first four of six years that we go. I find Floortime OT, the modality that teaches me the most about how to understand and interact with Joey. It is so helpful that we go for twelve years. I learn how to join him where he is and stretch his capabilities with playful obstruction and good humor. I learn how to have long non-conversations of back-and-forth silliness to grow his capacity for language. I learn the stages of emotional development, and how to support him at any level. I learn how to ask harder things of him when he's up to it. I learn how to recognize his early signs of needing a break, how to honor that and then pull him back into engaged play. I learn how to accept where he is in the moment and resist extrapolating his growth curve.

I find a private speech provider who we try for ten disappointing weeks before accepting that Joey will not engage with the people there.

Two therapy modalities are conspicuously absent here. I know ABA therapy is the gold standard, but early on Joey would literally shut down unless conditions were just right. My limited knowledge of ABA makes me think that Floortime OT is much better suited to him. Both types of therapy require so much time that I refuse to consider doing both.

Another modality I longingly and repeatedly look at is a developmental intensive for brain-injured children. If Joey was my only child, I may have done this. But I'm unwilling to give up my daily interactions with Joey's brothers, even for a few months. It sounds like a lifetime.

In addition to all this, I research heavy metal chelation and special diets and scores of supplements. I try what I consider to be the top five percent of the alternative medical treatments, including monthly day trips for a year to try chelation. As far as I can tell, they don't hurt but they don't help. The only correlations I find are that eliminating dairy from his diet gives him much more energy and stops his perpetually runny nose, and that artificial food dyes make him rigid and joyless. I feel like I'm doing everything I can to help Joey start learning and developing in all realms. The feedback that I get from others is that it looks like a lot.

LOOKING BACK

Joey makes quick judgements about people that rarely reverse. He either likes you from the get-go or he doesn't. I noticed this from an early age, but it took me many years of watching him to believe it. His decision whether to like someone is so fast that it seems like he's using a sense that I can't see, an aura or vibration that tells him friend or foe, aligned or not.

At one point early in my search for what would help Joey develop, my husband and I had a conversation that I'll never forget. He asked me to explain my justification for all these appointments, the time and expense and opportunity costs in committing to this complex and intense course of action. I said I didn't know that any of it would work. In fact, we came to an understanding that this was for me, not for Joey. I had put my time, my analysis, and my heart and soul into creating the proposed plan, but I had no guarantees. I knew that if I didn't do this, I would be miserable. This was how I wanted to parent, and it may as well be called mom therapy, because I was the one determined to try it out.

With all the lengths I was willing to go to, I had to be the one to take care of Joey. I learned basic sign language, in both American Sign Language and Signing Exact English. I tried different restrictive diets with Joey to see how they would affect him. I hired babysitters from a pool of local OT students and trained them to do one-on-one Floortime work with him. We had an extreme division of labor under one roof, but it is what I wanted, and it worked for a long time.

MY TAKEAWAYS

1. I needed experienced OT and speech therapists to model interactions with Joey for me. I gained a better understanding of how he sees the world and how he operates in it.

2. It was much easier for me to defend the idea of "mom therapy" than to forecast that Joey would benefit from all his appointments -- especially as the years unfolded without significant or measurable progress.

3. Even though he still operates at about a two-year-old level, I strongly believe that Joey is more interactive and cognitively flexible than he would be without the lengths I went to when he was young.

4. I would have chosen more sleep over any of the therapies that we did. Joey just wouldn't sleep.

5. The best people to invite into my life help me have stronger relationships with my children -- therapists, babysitters, and friends.

Brothers: age 4 to 8

through his brothers' eyes

Joey has two brothers. His older brother, Adam, is acutely aware of the discrepancies in abilities and behaviors between Joey and other kids Joey's age: kids at school, in the neighborhood, the gym daycare, and the younger siblings of his good friends. When Adam is six years old he knows that four-year-old Joey is kicked out of our neighborhood preschool's twos class with their little brother Thomas for lack of participation, even though Joey is not a bother. Adam is aware that we leave fun outings because Joey can't handle it, or because I can't handle Joey. He knows that Joey has lots of babysitter time where they do the stuff we learn at Floortime OT. Eight-year-old Adam knows how to be a Floortime play-partner even though it's hard work for him to focus only on Joey's infant-stage interests – moving and balancing on swings and watching a puppy puppet with a long tongue. Adam likes memorizing flags of the world and winning at chess and creating silly dances.

Joey's younger brother Thomas knows that he has two very different older brothers, and that he gets different things when he is with each of them. When Thomas is out with dad and Adam, they drive to the science center or walk to a movie theater or take a trip on an airplane. When Thomas is out with mom and Joey, they drive to therapies or grocery stores or walk to the park. One day Thomas says to me, "Mom, Joey can do anything, right?" I am momentarily silent. What can I say to this? "Well." Pause. "Yes, he can." Pause. "What… are you… noticing?"

Thomas's replies teach me a lot about what's important to him as a four-year-old. "Joey can sit on the rope ladder. I can't. It hurts my bum." Yes, Joey does that all the time.

"What else do you see?" I ask.

"Joey can eat a jalapeno bagel."

Wow. True. Recently I let the kids each pick their own bagels out of the bins at a grocery store and Thomas thought he was getting a cinnamon raisin bagel. I hadn't noticed the mix-up or I would have stopped him from taking a bite. His eyes welled up with tears, and I thought steam was coming next. I had to convince him to spit it out in my hand. We gave the rest of the bagel to Joey, who ate it right up, while I hugged Thomas on the floor in front of the cake counter.

With all the lists that I've been asked to make for classroom and therapy goals, never had I considered adding sitting on the skinny wooden rung of our IKEA rope ladder or eating spicy foods. I feel schooled by Thomas, who notices obvious strengths in his big brother. Seeing six-year-old Joey through the eyes of four-year-old Thomas is thrilling to me. It hits me that Thomas is the only person I know that expects the world to contain a person like Joey. I wonder when he'll see more of what Joey can't do. I wonder how I can foster his delightful and innocent perspective within myself.

trading places

When Joey is eight and Adam is ten, Adam and I have a difficult conversation. My explanation of "what is wrong with Joey" has always been that he can't learn as fast as others. It sounds less dire and more relatable than anything else I've thought of. Adam takes this knowledge and asks me if I would trade places with Joey, so that he didn't have his disability anymore. My first instinct is to say yes, but I pause. This feels important. It's not about Joey.

"No. I wouldn't."

"Why!?" asks Adam, eyes wide and frowning at the same time.

"Because that would mean I couldn't be your mom. Being your mom and Joey and Thomas's mom is so important to me that I'll never put it at risk. It's the most important thing I can do." He looks at me sideways.

"Besides, Joey is okay. He can't learn as fast as others, but he's okay." I didn't yet know the intensity that Joey's self-injurious and aggressive behaviors were going to reach, but I would've had this same conversation, even if I knew what was to come.

"Well, I would trade places with him," says Adam standing up straight, chest out a little.

"That's amazing, Adam! What are you thinking?"

"Well Joey can't learn as fast as me. I'm ten and I know a lot already. So if we switched places, I'd start learning more slowly and he'd start learning faster. Then you could know him better."

I stop breathing.

"That's what you want, right mom? If Joey could tell you stuff, you could know him better." He looks up at me, eyebrows raised and mouth slightly open.

Oh my heart. This has got to be the sweetest thing I've ever heard. His not-quite-right understanding of Joey's differences and what is important to me come directly from my mouth. I swallow to stall for time; I will my tear ducts to close and my voice to stay steady.

"You know, Adam, I tell you and Thomas how important it is to know you because you guys are the ones who need to hear it. You're both going to learn how to hide yourself from me. In fact, I'm already teaching it to you. When you get a present, we've taught you to say thank you, and add something positive, even if you don't really like it. That's a polite way of hiding your true self. As you get older, you'll get better and better at this, and you'll want to keep some things private for yourself and not share them with me. That's okay. But I want you to know for sure, in your heart, that I don't have a particular way I need you to be. You can think any thoughts and feel any feelings. For me, the most important part of being your mom is getting to know who you really are."

Adam looks at his feet and squirms. I continue on.

"If we could do any of these brain switches that we are imagining we'd really have to think this through. But we can't. I'm so happy I'm your mom, and I'm so happy you are you. I'm happy that Joey is Joey and Thomas is Thomas. I wouldn't have it any other way. In fact, do you think Joey likes himself?"

"Yeah," says Adam.

"Me too."

I know Adam needs to hear this. I leave unsaid how dearly I want to understand and treat Joey's condition. Adam already knows by how I spend my time.

Adam's love for me, for his brother, and even for himself is undeniable. He's such a solid kid. I'm glad that I told him I intend to be there for him and his brothers no matter what. When one kid needs so much more than the others the idea of fairness is especially skewed. I need him to know that he and Thomas are as important as Joey.

LOOKING BACK

While researching child development I looked at data for families with working parents, even though I was a stay-at-home mom or working part time. While trying to improve Joey's developmental trajectory, being his mom was like a full-time job. The research showed that, with short amounts of targeted time, infants know who their parents are and have a strong bond, even if others are doing the bulk of direct care. I took this snippet of information and made sure to have at least ten minutes a day of one-on-one time with each child. I took it a step further and tried to make sure to do Floortime activities with them: let them lead, meet them where they are in the moment, and go for the gleam in their eyes.

For our family, we used the "divide and conquer" strategy of parenting multiple children with different needs. I was afraid of making Adam and Thomas feel resentful of Joey, or worse: responsible for any harm that might come to him. We were often all together but I limited what I asked of them in relation to Joey. I made sure most of our activities with all three boys were fun: going to the park and climbing, dance parties at home, shared treats. Adam and Thomas were thriving physically and academically. Their dad was the primary parent for reading books aloud, playing games, exploring the city, and for help with their schoolwork. Looking back, it's clear that I always prioritized individual relationships over the group. I didn't decide this because I didn't want family time, I did it because I could see that it was what our kids needed for their optimal growth.

MY TAKEAWAYS

1. I strove for the best development possible for each child. I leveraged their preferences and took into account their temperaments and learning habits, their levels of energy and intrinsic motivation.

2. I strove for strong relationships with each of my children at the expense of working on the family as a whole. This was born from my observation of our needs and processes, not from devaluing the family unit at the outset.

3. I did my best not to rely on my typical children as part of my affected child's medical/safety/teaching team. This is in part a reaction to my inflated sense of responsibility for my own siblings. I do not pretend to know what is ideal.

4. Every day I spent a minimum of ten minutes alone with each of my children, where I followed their lead. It dropped off as they didn't want that time with me. As my neurotypical boys grew up, I prioritized being available whenever they spontaneously wanted to talk, plus frequently initiating short "difficult" conversations about values.

Acceptance: age 8

building a relationship in extreme circumstances

I wake up to see 2:06 a.m. on our digital clock and hear Joey bumping around in his bedroom. He is eight years old and often can't sleep through the night. He hasn't yet wiggled his doorknob, which I outfitted with a jingle bell bracelet so I can hear when he leaves his room. My feet find my jeans on the hardwood floor and I pull them on under my nightgown. I push my arms and head through a quarter-zip fleece and my gray-brown hair goes up in a ponytail. I make it into Joey's room and close the door behind me. I feel victorious that I am so far unnoticed by my husband or our other two kids, all sleeping. I sit next to Joey's bed, and with a soft slow descending tone I say, "Lay down." What would be rife with negative connotation to another person is just what Joey needs to hear in order to process language.

We bought a low, simple bed frame when Joey started climbing and jumping on his bed. We replaced his hanging ceiling light once he could make it swing by batting it with a pool noodle. As it nears 3 a.m., Joey stands in front of his closed door and knocks. I know this is the most polite way he can declare his intent, so I give up on getting him back to sleep. Time for us to go downstairs.

The bulk of our unfinished basement is a playroom with five escape routes. Doors connect to the garage, the backyard, the laundry room, the furnace room, and the staircase leading back upstairs. Plastic shelving divides the far end into a gaming retreat. In the main area, between the return pipes below the ceiling, sits a custom steel frame where we can hang swings, a rope ladder, or a punching bag. I have a crate of old VHS tapes from my nieces and a low cabinet housing a TV and VCR.

Joey looks content while he sits and rocks on the rope ladder. He's chewing on a stuffed turtle and watching "Kipper the Dog" animated episodes that I set up for him. With pillows and a down comforter, I settle in on the floor. I'm stationed so that I'll be bumped awake when he heads to the kitchen. The voice of the British narrator lulls me to sleep around 4 a.m. In my light drowse, I feel or hear the drop in atmospheric pressure. Cold air knocks my face awake. The first thing I see is the open door to outside and I realize Joey is gone. *Holy shit – he can reach the lock!* I jam my feet into my tennis shoes, laces splayed out, and bolt into the backyard, already bright with the motion-activated flood lights. I pause and slowly turn my head to listen for him. I can't hear anything over the chirping birds. *Where are you?* I don't yell because he won't answer or come. I lurch up the driveway, lit by a bright streetlight. Joey isn't under our dim porch light, caked with cobwebs. *He walks to things he likes.* On the side-walk I look right, the direction for muffins, but see no one. I go left, ten big steps, and there, next to the neighbor's porch swing – *thank you god* – stands barefoot Joey. I sit him down and feel that his hands are warm, his feet are cold but not icy. I step out of my shoes and put them on his feet and cinch up the laces. I take time to pick our steps back, me barefoot and trying to keep Joey's little feet from stepping out of my giant shoes. On our driveway, I smell the sweet vanilla plants that hedge our yard. Inside the closed door, I wrap him in my comforter and face him.

"Joey wants to go outside. Mama says... NO," I say while pointing and signing. He watches the door, doesn't look at his feet in my big shoes, or me.

"Joey wants to…," I prompt.

"Go," he says.

"Mama says…," I wait for him.

"NO," we say together.

Arms straight at his sides, he tips toward me on his toes. He lowers his chin to lean his forehead on me. He lets me play with his thick, messy hair. I am relieved that I found him, relieved that he is compliant and cuddly, not defiant and aggressive.

I wipe off our feet and take him upstairs to a warm bath. I'm still upset with myself that he was able to get outside. The echoes of my fear pulse through my head, as if I had been calling his name. Joey is warm and dry at 4:35 a.m. – one hour until our coffee shop opens, two hours until the others wake up, four hours until Joey's school bus comes.

LOOKING BACK

It was easy to lean into Joey's hugs and to help him choose different types of swings; it was hard to have so little sleep. It was easy to love and appreciate his sense of humor; it was hard to see him do repetitive movements that others describe as aimless. It was easy to learn from our favorite therapists and feel like I had community for a few hours a week; it was hard not to have friends who understood what we were really going through. It was easy to be proud of all my kids; it was hard to know how much time to spend with each of them.

I knew that my modifications to our life were atypical, but I accepted them. I would keep adjusting. I was being me: trying to be the best mom I could to all my children.

Joey didn't sleep much but I always tried to protect the sleep of his brothers and his dad in hope that they could thrive. I napped during the day when I could. Lack of sleep at night eventually prevented me from holding a part-time job, even while the kids were all in school. For me, a chronic lack of sleep resulted in reduced cognitive abilities, weight gain, and bouts of depression and anxiety.

MY TAKEAWAYS

1. Built environments and architecture can improve Joey's experience. Better structures where he can safely explore and climb allow for less direct handling, more outdoor time, and more experiences that are pleasant to his senses.

2. Safety during both day and night is improved with door alarms.

3. I felt like a martyr when Joey was young. It felt good for a short time, a real badge of loyalty and hard work. But it's unsustainable and isolating.

4. How important is my own health? I valued it more once I realized that my children would grow up to repeat my actions or expect similar from their future partner.

Isolation: age 9

something I wish to be true

"How the hell will I think of something to be grateful for by next week?"

A week before Thanksgiving, I ask my younger brother this, without a hint of sarcasm. He cracks up, joyful that his perfect, optimistic big sister is joining him on the dark and cynical side. I have no idea when I last felt thankful. I know I'm lucky in many ways, but I don't feel it. I love my husband and three kids. I work hard to help Joey navigate challenges due to his neurodevelopmental disorder. I'm living my values and priorities. But as my own abilities fall short of my goals, all of my relationships suffer: my marriage, my friendships, my parenting, my relationship with myself. I can't give anyone in my family all the attention they deserve. I can't live as I did before Joey's delays. And the biggest problem of all, the one that eclipses everything: no one can help me cure my son. Every thought I have about myself is steeped in disappointment. I have enough energy to hide it most of the time. But this Thanksgiving, I find that I can't feel gratitude. I don't know what I'll offer as my thanks at the dinner table, but I know it'll be something I wish to be true, not something I feel.

LOOKING BACK

An unfortunate consequence of my misery was that I pulled away from the people who care about me. I forced myself to go out to see friends about once a month, but I felt far away, different than I had before. When I smiled along with their typical stories of challenge and triumph, I tried to engage, but my own disappointment and grief were too strong. I felt truly alone despite being surrounded by people who cared.

MY TAKEAWAYS

1. When I was around Joey and he was happy, I felt fine.

2. When Joey was dysregulated, I felt scared, frustrated, confused, and helpless.

3. When I was away from him, I felt the sorrow and fear associated with his challenges.

4. Some days really sucked for me.

5. Some months really sucked for me.

Guilt: age 11

when victory is mistaken for failure

I tried to pick up Joey's prescription medicine yesterday, when a babysitter was working with him, but it was out of stock. I need the refill right now. We have a two-hour drive to his overnight camp and a mandatory check-in window. Joey loves camp, and this is my only chance for a few consecutive nights without him. I know he might have a tantrum once we go in the store; the question is, how bad will it be? I wish he could be safe in the car by himself. He's eleven years old and watching his iPad in the back seat. But the front car doors don't have child locks. He might leave the car and get lost or injured. I call the pharmacy from the parking lot. They have the refill ready, but they won't deliver it to my car. We'll have to run in together.

We round the aisle at the back of the store and see there's no line at the counter. Joey pulls on my shirt, his initial objection to joining me on my errand.

"I know you don't want to be here," I say, turning to check for other shoppers. *Neither do I.*

The clerk retreats to fetch the prescription.

"First medicine, then camp," I say to Joey. Without looking at me, he replies by moving his open hand over his head and lowering it toward me. My forearm redirects his mild protest. While I decline a pharmacist consult, Joey lets out one brief scream. *Here we go.* He raises his hand over his head again. I sidestep this heavy swipe and drop the pills into my purse. I envelop his hitting hand in both of mine and we retreat. *Done. Get back to the car.*

"Camp," I say, pulling him forward to lengthen his steps a little, his sturdy athletic shoes slapping the floor. He's walking, so I can tell he's resigned to getting himself back outside. Now he presses the back of his other hand against his front teeth, eyes darting and searching even though I'm right in front of him. I scan the store, looking for what he might be reacting to, and come up empty. We exit into the bright sun on a cool day. *We made it.* My car is about 200 feet away. Joey jerks and uses his molars to bite the back of his hand. I pull his hand away from his mouth while we keep walking. His eyes are open wide, looking hard toward the car. My forearm drifts near his mouth, and he bites me. I gasp and pull both his hands over his head. His jaw chomps the air. He looks pissed. He twists away from me. We are sidestepping, like dancing puppets. He continues to lift and lower each foot in turn. *He wants to get to the car, or he would sit down.* I focus on my car.

When his butt hits the third-row bench seat, he's no longer upset. He looks out the window, his forehead resting on the glass. Except for the red teeth marks on his hands, there's no lingering sign of our problem. I advance an inch at a time to reach into the back, where Joey lets me buckle his seat belt. I exhale. Through the rear window, I notice a slight woman standing behind my car. She's bent over, using her thigh to write something on a small piece of paper. *What is she doing? She's going to report me.*

"Hi!" I snap up out of the car and take brisk steps to offer her a hand-shake, as if that would help. When her shaky backpedaling stops a few yards back, she squints at me. *She thinks I am going to hurt her.*

"What are you doing? What were you writing?" I ask, hands now pulled back to my hips, feet wide, facing her. *She is planning to call Child Protective Services.*

"You would treat a dog better than that," she sneers.

I picture border collies herding cattle. I search for words that'll absolve me of the crimes she's imagined.

"Joey's fine now. He didn't want to be in the store. I had to get his medicine."

My voice sounds pinched. My choppy sentences accelerate.
"He's a great kid. He just didn't wanna be in the store. Please come meet Joey," I finish, drawing back a step while bending to reach out my hand. I don't expect her to look in on Joey. *I need a doctor's note about the tantrums.*

The Not-So-Good Samaritan looks between my license plate and the note in her hand.

"Just call the police now." I hear that my voice sounds low and deliberate. "They can sort this out. I'm not hurting my son. Just call the police."

She shifts her weight back and questions me with her face. *She thinks I'm abusive and crazy.*

"I think it's going to be okay," says an older, short-haired woman who has just appeared. Her blue jeans and untucked flannel shirt were stylish in the '90s. Her back and elbows lean against her small pickup truck. Her body is angled toward the store, and her palms face out. *De-escalation stance.* She isn't looking directly at either of us, but evaluates the situation.

"I think it's going to be okay," she repeats a little louder, in an even cadence.

"I don't think it WILL be okay for me," I say. "This woman's gonna report me to CPS."

"Well, I didn't say that!" says the Not-So-Good Samaritan, now flustered.

Her head turns back and forth between me and the calm woman, who asks, "How's your boy doing?"

"He's fine now that he's back in the car. He has autism plus intellectual disability. He doesn't like being in the store." I try to sound loving over my panic. Ms. Not-So-Good crumples the paper and shoves it in her pocket and looks around at the ground.

"Well, you should treat him better," is her parting shot at me, and she walks toward the store entrance. My face is worried, and my feet are stuck. When she passes the RedBox DVD rental vending machine, the adrenaline leaves my body – *thunk* – wet sand dumped from a beach pail.

I say thank you to the woman at her truck, breathy with veneration. Her hand dismisses me and my gratitude with an anemic backhand slap of the air.

I want to be driving away. I want to be looking through trees over rocky beach to the calm water in the inlet.

"Let's go to camp," I say to Joey, and close the sliding door. I walk around to the driver's side, studying the activity in the parking lot. I am numb. I reverse out of the parking space at a crawl, afraid of making any mistake.

LOOKING BACK

MISIDENTIFIED GUILT

I felt a huge amount of guilt when this stranger judged my parenting in the parking lot. Later I realized that what I felt was a combination of humiliation, shame, anger, and disappointment. It was not guilt because I knew I was doing all the right things in a tough situation. In fact, our outing was ultimately a victory – Joey successfully went to camp and loved it. But to an observer unfamiliar with our situation, my actions looked like a grave failure in parenting. I looked abusive. That judgment hit my highest-held value: being a good mom.

Guilt is supposed to mean deserving blame for offenses. I often felt guilty about not being able to help my sick child. This was not actual guilt. This was anger at the world, disappointment in the medical system, denial of my limitations, grief that I pushed away. It was common for me to feel guilty about not being in multiple places at once. This was not guilt. This was either disappointment in the laws of physics or impossible expectations that I failed to reject. Why do I label things as guilt that are not? I personally have found it more acceptable to place blame on myself than to feel or address my unrelenting anger, disappointment, and grief. By labeling it as guilt, I can cling to the idea that I could exert control over it, stop it with my behavior. I'm clinging to my huge sense of responsibility for Joey's wellbeing. But defaulting to guilt costs me my self-esteem, and I am the only one who can make it stop.

RISK

Helping Joey navigate the world safely involved sporadic moments of difficulty. I felt risk while doing normal things. He might run if I gave him more than a few feet of space. He might lash out at me or bite his own hands if he was especially frustrated or anxious. He might get injured. Or, much of the time, we had a lovely time together as I anticipated and accommodated his needs. I felt that my actions made all the difference between a peaceful outing and one with aggressive or self-injurious behaviors. It was easier to believe that it was all in my control, rather than face the uncertainty and randomness of everything that could happen. I could not see that there would be some bad outings, no matter what I did.

SHAME

As Joey's behaviors escalated, my brain got desensitized to his mild and frequent acts of aggression and self-injury. I stopped seeing them as a stranger does. I accepted that he communicated by biting his hand lightly or calmly grabbing my shirt or hair. I only worked at avoiding his more intense behaviors.

When I was constantly being brave in the face of increasing risk, it was hard to see the line between reasonable and unreasonable actions. Despite all my work anticipating his needs, I still found myself in situations where I only had bad options. Like when I pulled his hands over his head when he bit me in the parking lot: should I have let go of him, instead? Maybe, but he might've run away from me. He was pretty fast, and in a parking lot on the corner of two busy streets. It didn't seem safer. Should I have asked a stranger to help me? Perhaps, but I didn't trust a stranger when things were calm, and I didn't have the optimism that anyone would be helpful once the situation was out of control.

I felt shame that this was my life, not guilt that I had done the wrong thing.

MY TAKEAWAYS

1. Negative emotions are useful when used to process an event or enact change. But after that, the excess emotion pools in self-reproach.

2. I accuse myself of guilt instead of facing less acceptable emotions, like anger and shame.

3. Laughter in community is the antidote to anger, frustration, and disappointment.

4. Honesty and empathy within a loving community is the antidote to shame.

Fear: age 12

what Joey needs

At twelve years old, Joey is still obsessed with elevators, even though we never go ride them anymore. I started taking him on glass elevators at age two to work on his vision, his vertical saccade, where your eyes follow something moving slowly past and then snap back to watch the movement again. For years, I leveraged his interest in elevators and escalators into motivation to communicate with me, drawing out any vocalizations or signs he could produce. But last year, he started demanding them more forcefully even while enjoying them less. This summer, with school out and no babysitters who can handle him, his demands grow even more frequent, and they often morph into screams of terror.

Now Joey asks for elevators throughout each day. I say no and redirect him. When he is especially upset about anything at all, he fixates on elevators, and they become part of his tantrum. Sometimes he can say or yell "ella" but usually he signs his version of elevator over and over. He makes a wall with his hands, elbows out. The backs of his hands face me, fingertips touching, looking like elevator doors. He raises and lowers them as a unit. As his anxiety escalates, he bites the backs of his hands, and when I block him, he bites me. He pulls my hair and scratches me. To prevent the worst of the self-inflicted bites, I hold him down on his bed, as his doctors advised me, to keep his hands away from his mouth. I put a thick comforter between us, to protect us both. We both get mad and overheated. I can't find a way out of this pattern. His bite wounds take longer to clot. They get infected.

I'm red faced and sweaty and sections of hair are pulled out of my elastic band. It is 10:30 p.m. and I'm outside Joey's bedroom, holding the door closed. I'm on the phone with my favorite on-call nurse, Jan. She conveys caring along with concise expertise. During the call, she can hear him scream, hear him knock on the door, hear him yell "Ella." She already knows about the bite to my finger, the hair pulling, the scratch on my face. She knows it's been over 45 minutes of this and I'm scared. She knows most days include an hour or more in crisis and she knows I am desperate for help. "Are you safe?" she asks, like every call before. I am terrified of confessing my basic parental failing, but I need solutions. I don't know what could possibly help, but I have to try.

"No," I answer for the first time. "I don't feel safe and I don't know how to keep Joey safe either."
She doesn't have any new suggestions.
I let out a bitter laugh.

My late-night confession of powerlessness set something in motion, though, and the next day I realize we might get help in the form of funding. We've applied for in-home services many times, and have always been denied. This time, on our behalf, the clinic social worker prepares two applications to the state, one for in-home help and one for group home placement. She knows that the state opened a short window for emergency funding. We must submit the lengthy applications today.

Three weeks later, a new state caseworker calls to tell me of a letter that is traveling to my home address. It denies monetary support for in-home care for Joey, the latest denial in a long list of rejections.

Instead, he tells me the only way we can all be safe is for Joey to be placed in a group home, with a few other boys and shift workers. They will give full support to Joey. I get a meeting scheduled, but I am stunned and can't understand the offer.

We bring Joey to the caseworker's office. With his iPad and mango juice, I predict we may have 30 minutes to talk. We learn the particulars: there is only one opening in our county, and we can take it or leave it. Another will come up at some unspecified time in the future. I ask three times in a row to hear again the explanation of how three disabled and behaviorally difficult boys live safely in a house where no adult lives. I listen to the case worker patiently repeat that there are three shifts of workers, round-the-clock care. My husband is ready to try something new since our life is not working. I am terrified of injuring Joey while blocking his self-injury or defending myself from his aggression. I am equally terrified of losing control of the hundreds of decisions I make about him every day. The choice is to keep my illusion of control or give up all control. I don't want him to move. What I want is the power to help him develop. But this move is the only option I can see for a change in our pattern, for a chance at improvement.

"Will you accept the Voluntary Placement Program for Joey?"
I move first to sign the paperwork.

We go home and I stay glued to Joey. No matter where we are or what we do, I find it difficult to talk or play. I am paralyzed, imagining him without me. He still has devastating tantrums. I've been coached to put him alone in his room at the very first sign of trouble and hold the door closed. I remove myself unless his hands are bleeding from self-biting.

A month of waiting later, we drive for an hour through dismal rain, to check out the house. As we proceed down a dirt driveway, through pine trees at least 30-feet high, I know Joey will love this location. A quarter mile from the road, we park with four other vehicles. The dumpy 1980s ranch house has a mossy roof and a tall chain-link fence around the backyard. The property is on nearly an acre of land. They want to give Joey the biggest bedroom, with its own full bath. I can't imagine a less attractive house, or a more perfect setup for him. Lena, the house manager, shows us around. She is older than me, taller than me, with a German accent. During her shifts, she cooks for the house and drives the boys to their appointments. She laughs at my concerns about Joey eating enough and says she can fatten him up right away. The other caregivers are quiet. They sit with the clients in the living room. We talk about aggression; they are not worried. *Usually no one thinks they can handle him.* I am half devastated and half in awe. We are told we can move him in a few weeks. With bureaucratic delays, a few weeks turns into three numb months.

Moving day arrives. The caseworker recommends, in the strongest terms, that I must stay away for three full days, for Joey to acclimate. On day four, at my first visit, I am told that he has quit biting. "That's wonderful!" I gush and mean it. *He is happier without me.* I grab him in a hug and turn to hide my tears from Lena.

I decide to visit twice a week. My new goal is to reinforce his communication by giving him everything he asks for, except elevators. It's a short list with a few foods, songs, and activities. Joey cracks up every time I sing his favorite lyric from "Aquarium," with a silly underwater effect. We eat orange chicken and cake pops. We seek out a new pool, a new playground, a new beach. When he attempts to say and sign, "I love you, bye bye," I know he's dismissing me, and I leave with an "I love you," a hug and a smile. I wait until I'm on the dirt driveway to sob.

Over a few months, his scabbed hands heal into scars. Joey starts at a new school, one with much more infrastructure to handle his need for movement. They even have a large tricycle that he can ride inside the school. I'm amazed at how great the move is for him.

Nine years have passed since he moved, and I am crying yet again as I write this.

LOOKING BACK

The fact that Joey is calmer and safer in a group home is wonderful, as that was my goal for him. I'm still surprised that it helped. It's also devastating to me. I must come to terms with the excruciating reality that the environment he currently needs in order to thrive is away from me. By trying to look at the world from Joey's point of view, I can think of several ways in which his new environment helps him.

I have the sense that the visual world can be too much for Joey. When Joey lived with us, I drove him around a metropolitan area to schools and stores, parks and therapists. He always got in the car and seemed to like it, except for some incredible tantrums at certain intersections. Now he sees much less of the world per day, mostly just home and school, which reduces his visual overwhelm.

Joey is particularly good at motor planning: moving his body around in space. At the group home, he is home a lot. Movement is his activity. Doctors describe it as aimless, but I don't think Joey feels that way. He likes being able to go to the back yard and then return to his room; he likes being in charge of himself. When he lived with us he spent more of his time in the car, riding where I decided to drive, or being ushered through the community by me.

Joey has a limited capacity for task demands, and he has a limited work tolerance. Now when he pops into the living room and says hi to people watching TV and runs right back to his room, they celebrate him for being social. I would've asked for a more sustained interaction. While in my care, people were in his face, handling him, asking things of him. His life at the group home is much more relaxed.

I have the sense that Joey views me as a tool to get what he wants. I am a fun, complex, and accommodating tool. I understand more of his requests than other people, and so he expects more from me. I think that constant proximity to the get-all-the-things tool causes him anxiety. Having visits with me allows him to get all he wants from me for a time, but that time ends. I respect his choices on what we do and when our visit is over. His anxiety doesn't build.

While I do not regret my intense work with Joey as a child, I can see that his teenage years were bound to be different. In retrospect, I think that his tantrums were communicating his need for a major change, not for me to make hundreds of small accommodations each day.

Am I deluding myself that Joey is happier because he needed less visual stimulus and more freedom to roam? Maybe. Maybe he remembers how he felt every time I restrained him or wouldn't give him what he wanted. Maybe he is happy to visit me but not to live with me. While I dearly wish I knew Joey's thoughts, I simply do not. My thoughts outlined above are based on my observations, and they support my relationship with Joey. That's what matters the most to me. I have a profound, flattening sense of disappointment that I couldn't give Joey what he needed for a good life in my home. I've done what I can, which is to give him a good life not in my home. The move to a group home was the right decision for us. While I'm still sad, I know we are terribly lucky. The unmet need for residential care for people with developmental disabilities is inhuman. Many families need full-time or respite care and get no services at all. Many are left to call for help from first responders. I have the privilege of feeling my feelings instead of living in ongoing crisis.

MY TAKEAWAYS

1. After Joey moved, I was left wondering "What if I'm okay while he's not okay?"

2. It took me a long time to see the error in my thinking. Joey is okay.

3. Good health is not owed to any of us. Joey might not learn to talk or dress himself. He might remain underweight and develop other medical issues.

4. I am always more successful at helping Joey when I am happy and healthy.

5. People often say they will do anything for their child. We conjure up feats of strength and self-sacrifice within our typical family structure.

6. It was much harder for me to give up our family structure than I can say.

Connection: age 19

building a relationship in new extreme circumstances

The spring that Joey turned 19 was when his high school abruptly shut its doors due to the global pandemic. One month into our state's lockdown, I receive a photo of him from the house manager that makes me laugh and cry at the same time. The photo shows him that morning, in a hammock in his sunny backyard, leaning out and looking at a laptop screen on the ground. He's in a virtual class with his special-education teacher and classmates. "Here he is," I think, "doing something I had no idea he could do." His house manager set up the meeting and brought her laptop outside because he wouldn't stay at the dining room table to participate. Who knows how long he stayed in the meeting? It's wonderful to note his progress, but bittersweet to not see it in person. I'm tickled that he happens to look "normal" in this photo, and a little disappointed that I still have the notion that normal looks a certain way.

Like everybody else with a loved one in a long-term care facility, I was unable to visit Joey for the first few months of the pandemic. Once I realize that he can participate in a video meeting, we set up a call on his iPad. I am overjoyed to see him rocking back and forth in a rocking chair, smiling, and asking me for his favorite songs through sign language and some utterances. He stays engaged for a full hour. I think each of us is tired but unwilling to be the first to go. The next day is the same but on the third day, he finds the "Stop Camera" button. Every time his caregiver starts the camera, Joey turns it off. He doesn't complain or tantrum, he doesn't say bye or just get up and leave. He rocks way back and starts a low belly chuckle, and slowly leans forward so his outstretched index finger turns off the camera. His laughter increases when the camera shuts off. I'm a little disappointed that he doesn't want to interact with me, but I'm elated to hear his laughter. It even feels right to witness his mildly oppositional teenage behavior.

For seven years, I've been visiting Joey at the series of homes where he gets support for all aspects of living. The first one closed due to the low number of staff and a series of on-the-job injuries. The second was always supposed to be temporary because it provided a higher level of care than he needed, although it ended up lasting six months rather than the predicted few weeks. Joey will be moving from his current home to an adult-based home by his 21st birthday. Our visits have always been organized around me driving him to whichever restaurant or outdoor location he wants. Whatever we do, I work on our communication and loving connection. I quiet my brain to enjoy sitting with him. In our conversations, I wait longer in hopes that he can process his thoughts. Sometimes I'm rewarded by seeing his authentic ideas, or his intrinsic motivation. My agenda is to get to know him better, to find humor, to enjoy what he enjoys.
It's working.

When Joey indicates he wants a particular park, we go. Sometimes when I open his car door, he clutches the seatbelt crossing his chest, indicating he will not get out. I used to feel like a failure when this happened, and I didn't know what to do next. Did I misread him, is this my mistake? Should we drive away? Or if I let him stay in the car when he said he wanted to be here, will I reinforce miscommunication? Should I haul him out? My fear mirrored the intensity of my desire to help him learn. Encouraging and reinforcing his heartbreakingly infrequent communication has been my priority for his whole life. Now on the occasions that he clutches the seatbelt I ask him: "Do you want to drive away?" If he says "go" or "car," or points toward the front windshield, we drive. If he looks out the side window I wait a bit, content that he is calm. After a minute I ask, "Do you want to walk? Or sit and talk?" Once in a while he's ready to get out of the car. More often, he wants to stay in the car and talk. We currently enjoy facing boats in the marina, sitting near 40-foot-tall trees at the park, and lingering outside his work training program at the school district complex. I keep my tone upbeat, my pacing slow, and note things in the present moment. I might point out someone walking a dog or branches waving in the breeze, and he may or may not notice them. Sometimes I guess at what he is thinking about and ask if he is thinking about that or "something else." "Something else" is a great category, it can keep the conversation moving forward. It makes for a slow game which usually ends in us laughing together.

I try to balance both new and familiar activities with Joey. It's not always clear what he wants, and since I initiate most of the choices, my decisions are highly influential. I aim for neutral emotions. While any parent likes to see their child happy, happier is not better for Joey. Too much excitement and too much anticipation overwhelm him. Whenever he looks and sounds as if he is in pain, I have to assume that he is uncomfortable. It's the same with work. Engaged activity is the foundation of work. Stretching the time he can be engaged is required for increased work, or "work tolerance" as it's referred to in school. My opinion on how much to push him has decreased dramatically. Now I base my expectations on my moment-to-moment observations of his emotions and behaviors rather than any past performance.

Today's visit starts in the typical way. I ask him a series of questions, offering two choices each time, until we arrive at a simple plan. We end up parked in a restaurant parking lot, off hours, next to the marina. We walk hand-in-hand from the car, about 30 steps, to a high, splintery wooden railing on the pier. I throw a fleece blanket over the rail to prevent him from getting slivers. We stand looking at our silhouettes on the water below. There's no breeze, no wake, and we have a nice long look. I don't quiz him or ask if he wants to throw rocks in the water. Shore birds fly by, and no other people are around. A few times he looks up at me and smiles, drumming his hands in approval. We stand next to each other, doing the same thing, having a restfully good time in nice weather. We've had many experiences that look similar to this from the outside. This time, our calm activity together isn't my second choice, after a more industrious or intense activity fails. This time, there's not even a twinge of sadness, shame, or disappointment. This time, I have a deep sense of peace.

All this success can start to feel heady, almost like Joey and I have no more issues. Our next experience is similar except for the ending. As I shepherd Joey from my car to his front door, I remember that I want to cut his fingernails. As a 19-year-old, he's less coordinated at walking and running than when he was young. He often stands still, waiting to take my hand or arm. I say "Joey, wait here. I want to trim your nails." While I fetch the clipper from my car, he surprises me by darting inside his house. I knock on the door and have him come back outside. We sit on the lawn while I trim all 20 nails. We have a system: I press a bit on each nail before I use the clipper, and I give him a break between snips.

When we are done, he signs wash, and I ask if he's talking about the car wash. "Yesh!" he affirms, leaning his upper body into the word. I say "Not today." Without warning, he stands up. I rush to stand also. I'm only halfway to upright myself when he grabs a hank of my hair right near the scalp. I freeze in my bent over state, my scalp in pain, listening to hairs rip out of my head. I yell for a staff member, who comes right out and helps Joey let go of my hair. The caregiver suggests I go, and I do. Joey will stop protesting my decision when I'm gone. He expects only me to take him to the car wash, no one else.

At a stoplight a mile down the road, I check my heart rate. It's still elevated. I run my fingers through my hair and at least 50 more hairs come out. What went wrong? I forgot that Joey doesn't show his displeasure in subtle ways. I forgot that current success, at the tricky job of trimming nails, doesn't guarantee future success, in the transition back inside his house. I forgot that every time he comes out of his house to see me, I take him somewhere in my car. His expectation was no different, even though we had just finished a visit the moment before, even though I asked him not to go into the house in the first place. It was a reminder that he needs a higher level of care than most people, and that our good times are not a given. It was a reminder that as hard as I try to see the world from Joey's point of view, I'm bound to my own ways of thinking. It takes constant effort to predict how he will think and act, and I won't always get it right.

LOOKING BACK

To have a great relationship with Joey I need to be at my best. I am consistently assessing how to plan time for us that will result in mutual feelings of connection. Some of that includes taking care of myself.

I still feel stress around the choices I make about how to spend my time. More visits with Joey? Or more hobbies, work, time with other family members? I make small and concrete decisions often rather than trying to plan too far into the future. That is how I keep on top of my feelings: I give myself the freedom to adjust.

MY TAKEAWAYS

1. I am the one who needs to learn and adapt. Joey keeps being himself.

2. Engagement with neutral emotions is my goal with Joey. His functional window is narrow and I'm always aiming for it.

3. I feel more pride in witnessing Joey's character than scrutinizing his benchmarks. I try to stay in gratitude when we are together.

4. When talking to Joey, I look for what he is thinking about. I match his energy, add light humor to upregulate, or give him time to calm.

5. My approach for our visits is to first ask for his input, then make him an offer, then read his response, and adjust or repeat.

Frustration: age 20

can we keep a dentist?

We have been asked not to return to five different dental offices due to Joey's aggressive and self-injurious behaviors when he is anxious or scared. The one place that is completely equipped to handle my now-adult son has a two-to-three-year wait list. With the help of my friends, I find a dentist that advertises serving people with special needs who is also accepting new patients. I set my expectations to Joey getting used to the exam room, maybe even a cursory look in his mouth.

I have been stewing in disappointment with the world -- a world unqualified to care for Joey. I'm bracing for a necessary event with a long history of struggle and pain for us both. I replay a distressing memory of getting him into a full body wrap and holding his head. His terrified eyes and strangled yelps plead with me, while a dentist counts his teeth.

We had previously experienced a freak set of scary moments when Joey had an X-ray and cavity filling at a special needs dentistry. While four of us struggled to get the mask blowing general anesthesia onto his face, the sedative accidentally doused me. So I started out woozy and mad.

Then I was horrified when I was told his heart rate dropped danger-ously low, prompting an intervention with a dose of atropine. Next, I felt sick and guilty while rushing him to see a cardiologist, as required by the private pre-paid anesthesiologist. And finally, I felt a combina-tion of relief, frustration, and confusion when the cardiologist chided me, saying he had neither needed to come in nor needed the atropine to raise his heart rate. What should have been a straightforward (if expensive) dentist appointment turned into an all-day roller coaster ride of ordeals.

I think clearly in urgent situations, but it takes me a long time after-wards to identify and address what I felt during the crisis. It's my peer group of moms of kids with extreme needs who help me step through the layers of emotions. Our lunches are long check-ins, and as I recounted these events, others chimed in with their own related stories. As I listen to their experiences and hear their reactions, I begin to understand details of my own emotional journey.

By text, the extreme moms wish me good luck with the new dentist appointment. They ask for updates when it's over.

I dress for a minor skirmish: my heaviest blue jeans, a long sleeve shirt and hoodie, my jog bra. I pull my shoulder-length hair back in two low pigtails, with barrettes to keep hair from falling forward into reach. I trim Joey's fingernails and my own so any scratches we get will be minor. I have snacks to curb his hunger, his favorite songs downloaded to entertain him, extra toothbrushes to occupy his hands and mouth. I have a sketchpad where I hand-draw simple pictures and words to prepare him for what will happen, just a few steps at a time. I already know that this dentist doesn't use any form of restraint. We'll have to build Joey's tolerance for an oral exam. It might take many visits. I know Joey best: I know his looks, his tolerances, when to push, and when to allow. I don't bring anyone else with me because I don't know anyone else who could reduce his anxiety around a new dentist. In the waiting room, Joey is quiet, sitting in a corner away from the other patients. I stand at the front of his chair, hemming him in. When I bend down, he grabs a pigtail, protesting that we are here, that we are waiting. "Safe hands. Open," I say with elongated vowels. I slow my breath while waiting for him to let go.

The staff exude positivity and kindness. Nevertheless, they do not comply with my most crucial request – communicated once on the phone during the appointment setup, again in the online paperwork, and again when we arrived. I want the dentist to examine Joey at the beginning of the appointment, when Joey's most likely to cooperate. We are led past the open exam area into the only private room, and Joey sits on the long, reclined chair and crosses his legs at the an-kle, looking relaxed. So far, amazing. The assistant stands behind the chair and starts clanking instruments and tapping drawers shut. Repeatedly Joey turns to the racket behind his head. He chews and chews on a toothbrush and drools a small amount of blood-tinged saliva. He runs a finger over two fingers on his other hand, his own characteristic soothing technique. The assistant is unaware of Joey's anxiety, unaware that he just uncrossed his legs. I'm wondering how best to keep Joey seated and compliant when he makes a move to start standing up. I put my hand gently on his chest.

"Can the dentist come in now and start?" I ask the assistant. She leaves the room. I stay very close to Joey, in full entertainer mode, and he stays seated. I am singing and signing and suggesting more songs with a pointed lack of embarrassment, even when she returns. "The doctor will be in soon, Joey is next."

Twenty minutes into the appointment, Joey's been anxious long enough. He stands up straight with a neutral face and turns toward the open door without a sound. At this moment the dentist enters and stops face to face with Joey. I say I'll talk to

Joey about sitting down. The dentist and assistant talk over each other, cajoling him back into the chair, to no effect. I get out the large sketch pad and draw a simple version of the dentist chair with the words SIT and COUNT. Below that, I draw an outline of a cake pop, which is in my backpack as his reward. Again, I ask them to just let me talk to Joey.

"First sit, and count teeth. Then, cake pop." I point to the pad as I speak. Joey isn't looking and doesn't answer. I move the drawing into his field of vision. I repeat it over and over, pairing the visual and auditory information for him in an even rhythm, looking for any response. I want to move this along, but he gives me no feedback. The stakes are high: I know that a tantrum will make a strong negative memory of this room, this office, this part of the city.

Despite not knowing his state of mind, I finally ask, "Do you want a cake pop?" If he answers no, we will leave. If yes, he's willing to sit again.

Joey remains silent. He looks at his hands and sits back down in the chair on his own. Success!

The assistant and I each hold one of Joey's hands while the dentist uses just a bite block and a little mirror to see and maneuver around his mouth. With my free hand, I hold the brown paper pastry bag above his head, and he gazes up, anticipating the treat inside. When he starts to struggle, the dentist pulls back and pauses. I ditch the bag and show Joey the pink sphere of cake on a stick, and he lets me press on his chest so his back rests on the chair again. The exam continues. When Joey stands up again, I help him communicate to the dentist and assistant that the exam is over. I hold out the treat and he devours it.

Joey silently ambles toward the open door. The dentist is talking to me, and I am stuck behind the big chair and rolling tray and people in this small room. I ask the assistant to slide the door closed and she does. As the dentist keeps talking, Joey inches the door back open. I free myself and slip between Joey and the door, blocking him from running to find the elevator in the parking garage that we glimpsed on the way in. Now I can listen to the dentist.

I struggle to understand how often this particular dentist recommends giving general anesthesia, which is necessary to complete Joey's X-rays and fillings. He doesn't realize that previous conflicting advice motivates my questions.

I am a bit giddy with relief due to the victory of a brief exam without restraint or drugs. I am also disappointed by the few deficiencies we experienced. As we leave, the dentist offers that the sketch book was amazing. *It's blank paper. I'm the one communicating with him.* I manage to push my defensiveness aside and take it as the compliment it was intended to be. I'm cautiously optimistic about trying this again.

LOOKING BACK

I know that community is important, especially when I am struggling. What exactly is community? I want it to be where I belong. There is the special needs community of families that I rely on, the women that know the details of our dentist appointments and cheer me on, and friends in our rare disease group. There is the special needs community of doctors and educators, people we rely on for expertise as well as the people who confuse us with conflicting advice. There is my family, my neighbors, and the entire world inhabited by Joey's typical siblings: people who support us, sometimes just in theory. No community is perfect. The people who have built me up and the people who have let me down are all mixed together in each of these groups.

The world is not set up for Joey and his anxiety, his emotional development, and his size and strength. Simple changes that are possible now would make a world of difference, like giving us a buzzer that beeps when the dentist is ready as if we were at a busy mall restaurant. Like fixing their ceiling video player and offering kid shows from the 2000s. Like taking me seriously when I say that he is leaving the room.

MY TAKEAWAYS

1. I prepare as much as I can for difficult outings. Afterwards, I try to let my frustrations go.

2. I can text my friends for support on everyday actions.

3. My friends remind me that everyone has their own myopic perspective.

Hopes: age 21

so what does he do all day?

I have spent nearly a decade trying to adjust to being the mother of a child living outside of my home. I have made some progress but mostly it feels wrong in my soul, and my brain is not proving powerful enough to change that. So when Joey turns 21, I am surprised to find that my discomfort begins to soften on its own.

A few things fall into place for me. The first is profound relief. For two years, I tried to facilitate Joey's move to a group home that serves adults, but we weren't offered an opening. I still am not a fan of the lack of control I have over his life now that he is cared for by a combination of state and federal programs. The month before he turns 21, the deadline when he is required to move out, Joey is offered a new placement. I am impressed by the head administrator who seems to have a great philosophy and a large, committed team of caregivers. I clear my schedule to meet with the service provider, visit the apartment and roommate, then bring Joey to see how he reacts, all on the same day. On the drive home I accept the placement on Joey's behalf. Over 200 people are considered for the spot that is offered to him. Historically, when there have been gaps in care, I have been the one to fill in, for either a few nights or up to six weeks. In the current climate of housing crisis and caregiver shortage I've been holding my breath, unsure if I'll be tapped in. Now I can relax.

When I move Joey into his new life, I decide to turn down the last two-and-a-half months of his eligibility for the school district job training program. I consider whether he'll get something meaningful from it. I imagine all the time and effort it will take for the staff to get to know Joey. I imagine his anxiety while getting used to a new school. The cost is too great for the benefit, especially since he has already had several years of job training with people who understand and celebrate him.

School has never been a place that was set up well for Joey. Yes, he has had some amazing teachers and programs. But he does not yearn to sort by color, or trace, or learn about calendars. A more amazing system would be living on a farm or a ranch where he could safely explore and do things meaningful to him, at a pace suited to him. Ideally, I would be able to set up a living tailored for him, not try to make him navigate the world as we have built it.

Joey's new home is an apartment complex with many townhome-type buildings on several acres. The grounds have a small playground, a dog park, and a pond with a fountain that he loves to watch and listen to. He has one of the bedrooms in a two-bedroom apartment to himself. He has his own bathroom and shares the living spaces with a roommate his age and general description. Joey and his roommate each have their own full-time caregiver for the 12-hour day shift. During the 12-hour night shift they share a caregiver (who stays awake).

I furnish Joey's apartment with typical IKEA furniture. The only unusual piece is a large stand supporting a swing chair in the living room. I supply door alarms when he moves in.

"So what does he do all day?" I tense up when someone asks me this because I anticipate they'll be disappointed with the answer. Joey takes his medicine at 8am and 8pm every day. That's his only scheduled activity for now. He has complete assistance at hand for all the activities we tend to do for ourselves: dressing, showering, preparing food, keeping the apartment clean. With his caregivers, he's working on learning the steps of doing his laundry and doing his dishes. With a caregiver he takes walks and goes to the store to choose his groceries. On his own, he naps, navigates his iPad, walks around in the apartment, sits in the swing chair, finds a favorite page in a book, and looks at his toys.

When I come to visit, once or twice a week, we do what Joey asks for. We often go to the car wash. We use the do-it-yourself soapy brush and water spray at one place, and then travel down the street for the vacuum at another place, because that's what he likes. I know what he likes because first he tells me with his signs and word approximations, then he confirms it with his participation and smiles.

During our visits, I always try to work in more vigorous outdoor activities. In the past, we've had success with a walk at the beach, where I hold his hand tight and keep him wading in the shallow water, or a park with shady trees, where I watch for mosquitos, or a track to practice for Special Olympics, where I keep us in an outside lane. I recently tried a series of rock-climbing sessions for people of all abilities and was thrilled that he was receptive and engaged. The organizer asked me if we were getting what we wanted out of it, perhaps prompted by Joey's meager progress. I gave her my unvarnished enthusiasm. "He is staying emotionally regulated in a new environment, even while waiting! … I know he loves it because he pulls his aide to the rock wall! … This is the most success we've had in years!" She takes it all down on her clipboard. I tell her I intend to work on right-left patterning with Joey and participate in the program again next year.

I rent a garage on a bike trail to house Joey's recumbent tricycle, and I buy a second trike for me and hitch them together like a train. During our first ride he is so happy that he smiles and sings the whole time. We ride to a playground where he does the slide a few times, very slowly, and then we ride back to the garage.

What Joey really wants is for me to take him to fast food. I rarely do this now that his caregivers shop and cook just for him. Earlier in the pandemic many a drive-thru kept us connected. Some of his most creative and robust ideas express his fast-food desires. On his own he co-opted the sign for "windy" for the burger joint Wendy's. After I took him to get a haircut next to a Panda Express, he started calling that location the haircut Panda. It took me many months to understand his demand for "beach." He wasn't happy with any of the beaches we went to, but one day in line at Taco del Mar he pointed to a photo of a beach and yelled "beach!" He had been asking for Beach Tacos all along. He communicates his food demands so clearly and delightfully that it is heart-wrenching for me to deny him.

Joey always wants me to sing, whistle, or play his favorite songs. At least two-thirds of his communications are song requests. Often, he asks for a new song just a few lines into the current one. His favorite songs include "Changes" by David Bowie (he signs change), "Hey Ya" by Outkast (he sings the notes to the title "aaaah aaaah"), "Sixteen Going on Seventeen" from the Sound of Music (he signs the number ten), "Jolly Holiday" from Mary Poppins (he signs apple on his cheek. I have no idea how or why he thought this one up). He has crushes on a wide variety of entertainers: Julie Andrews, Rihanna, and Leah from Signing Time™.

Joey continues to sign "elevator." Riding on elevators or watching elevator ride videos on YouTube brings him to his worst behaviors quickly, so we don't do it. I discourage other people from taking him near elevators.

I've always imagined my children would live independently from me as adults. I didn't have a clear vision of when "adult" would arrive for Joey. Age 18 was too early. I had more concerns then about his living situation and how he spent his days. Now that he has turned 21 it feels right. I didn't see that shift coming. I was too concerned about finding an environment that was reasonable for him. Now my sadness is lighter, and the guilt I carry is dissolving.

Joey no longer goes to school. He's more relaxed, and he gets to sleep when he wants. He's finally gaining weight, sleeping well, and enjoying new activities with me. These signs of wellbeing are reassuring, and they affect me deeply.

When I am with Joey, I give him all my attention and creativity. Then we both go to our separate homes.

LOOKING BACK

My hopes for the future are big. Even the ones that may sound small to others feel big to me. I hope daily that he'll learn to use a restroom, so we can have longer outings at more venues without the need to clean his clothes or the car due to incontinence. This would require building up slowly to an intensive behavioral program or an increase in bodily awareness. Someday I hope we'll enjoy a carousel ride without a meltdown. This would require him to be cured of his high anxiety. I hope that he'll have thoughts that he tells me about, that he'll have appropriate and gentle ways to advocate for himself, and that his sensory profile will be his ally instead of his enemy. I'm not sure this will ever be possible. I believe it would require the development of an effective treatment for Syngap1 haploinsufficiency.

Science is always moving forward, but not necessarily in time for us. The Syngap Research Fund (SRF) is a patient advocacy group that is accelerating treatments for people with Joey's ailment. SRF has generous and visionary co-founders, dedicated volunteers, amazing parents on the board of directors, and world-class professionals on their Scientific and Clinical Advisory Boards. SRF raises money, raises awareness amongst scientists and clinicians, funds targeted research projects, and brings affected families together to support each other. As a scientist I have many high hopes, but as the mom of an affected adult, I am eagerly anticipating drug trials that will find safe and meaningful treatments for some or all of Joey's symptoms.

I live the full range from catastrophe to bliss with my child with extreme special needs. When advocating for Joey I must include his ability to destroy, to assault, to harm himself. When I'm enjoying his sense of humor or I understand a new sign of his, I see his angelic self. When I'm dreaming of our future, I envision an architectural heaven that meets Joey's sensory and safety needs. It would give him appropriate challenges, independence, and keep him safe. I dream of finding him helpful treatments, jobs, and activities for us to do together.

Whatever happens, I know Joey will be himself.

MY CURRENT WORK

1. How can I honor myself and honor my child? What does that look like?

2. What can I give my child that no one else can?

3. My highest priority is Joey's safety. How can I stay in gratitude for it being achieved?

4. How soon can our best lives be built, and how can we both be okay in the meantime?

I was the one who had to learn

My parenting role expanded on the day after Joey's first birthday, when his delays were quantified in a diagnosis. Over the next few years, I became his researcher of treatments, special diet chef, speech and physical therapist, mischief-proofer of home and car, behaviorist, manager of the educational team at school, medic, and security guard. When parenting him, it was easy to prioritize the never-ending to-do list instead of focusing on our parent-child relationship. My relationships with Joey's brothers were built observing each other and creating connections. My observations of Joey were shrouded in the judgment of whether he was advancing or regressing. We shared a chronic lack of sleep that interfered with our ability to connect. He interacted with me and gave me feedback in unexpected ways that confused me. My personal connection to Joey, which should have been the most revered aspect of my parenting, fell to the bottom of the list in the face of his therapy goals, medical emergencies, and behavioral threats to his own safety.

When faced with all of Joey's challenges, my instinct was to work harder to help him develop. That strategy left me exhausted and defeated. I finally learned an empowering bit of wisdom: to be a great parent to Joey I must foster a sense of connection with him. When my connection to him is strong, I feel proud and at peace. It's a self-reinforcing cycle: when I feel proud and at peace, I access my intuition and feel our connection. Joey senses when I'm distraught, so building an authentic connection with him requires me to feel good myself. Saying abstract words to convince him of my pride and joy doesn't work. How was I going to consistently feel this good?

For many years, I resisted prioritizing my own wellbeing. I had bigger and more urgent issues to tackle just trying to improve Joey's prognosis and keep him safe. Here are a few of the excuses I told myself:

I'm fine. Between all the therapy appointments, schools, and regular life activities, I could not slow down enough to see that my negative self-talk weighed me down more than the packed schedule.

I don't need to feel better, I only need to help my child. This statement reveals the biggest flaw in my thought process. I can't improve our relationship by focusing only on Joey. By working on myself, I feel more gratitude and peace, which improves my energy and patience, both when he is happy and when he is emotionally dysregulated.

I already take care of myself! I had many opportunities each day to get a latte or read a magazine, but those common acts of self-care were not up to the extreme task at hand. I needed consistent sleep at night, exercise and nutrition during the day, caregivers capable of meeting Joey's complex needs, the time and energy to enjoy a hobby. They all sounded like luxuries to me because they were difficult or impossible to attain. Sometimes, the only meaningful self-care available to me was examining my thoughts and emotions.

I don't want to change myself, I want our situation to change! I was as surprised as anyone that shifts inside me could give me a sense of peace when our external situation – Joey's health and development – had not changed at all. Through examination of my thoughts, I found traps I had laid for myself that I fell into every time. Spending even small efforts toward understanding and nurturing myself has made me happier and more energetic. I feel more like myself.

I strive to be the best parent I can be for Joey. To do that, I need to create the best connection I can with him. For a strong connection, I need to feel lighthearted, grateful, and ready to start where we are. That is hard, especially when dealing with the constant grief that accompanies having a child who is struggling, a family whose shared life has been altered, and an unfamiliar identity. I find it all easier when I lighten my emotional burdens. Which emotions are burdensome? Here are some that affect me:

Pure sadness. I have a son who is unlike anyone else I have ever met. He is different because of a genetic typo, one letter different from his parents and siblings. He has medical and behavioral issues that deserve remedies. But there is no cure, and we are left to try inadequate treatments that address only a small fraction of his challenges. For these reasons, I carry a permanent deep sorrow within me. Over time, I can distance myself from the sadness, especially with distractions. But when I think about Joey's lifelong challenges and all the thoughts he cannot communicate to me, my grief is as powerful as ever.

Guilt shows up in many stages of parenting, whether or not it is earned. Intense guilt first appeared when I noticed Joey's delays. As he aged without developing, guilt flattened me: both when I wished him to be different than his precious self and when I felt responsible for his challenges. Guilt creeps in during conflict and indecision about how to allocate resources within our family, including when deciding on treatments and planning vacations.

Guilt is supposed to mean feeling sorry for an error. But for me, guilt around parenting ballooned into a diffuse malcontent at being powerless to change reality. Guilt masked a mixture of anger, disappointment, and shame. How do I behave when I feel bad about my actions or inactions? Not well. The price for holding on to chronic guilt is an erosion of my self-worth.

Isolation happened slowly for me. It started when Joey was not welcome in our neighborhood preschool with his brothers and continued when friends and family could not accommodate his needs. Physical isolation peaked as his behaviors became unmanageable for me or for anyone else. And a lonely desperation wrecked me because no one could help me accelerate his development. Looking back, there were times I was unwilling or unable to receive any comfort, even from those closest to me. Those mistakes further isolated me. Now I do my best to accept and appreciate the support being offered, even though it doesn't fix the situation. Our medical puzzle may be unsolvable for now, but we can survive it, and with support and connection, we can thrive.

LOOKING BACK

Paradoxically, the best (and often only) way for me to foster a strong relationship with Joey is to attend to my own emotional well-being. Specifically, I must find a way to relax and think deeply about my thoughts and emotions.

MY TAKEAWAYS

1. I am harder on myself than is helpful.

2. Taking time to feel okay, rather than enduring the helpless urgent chaos that rules my mind, helps my children as much as it helps me.

3. Nothing and no one can help me feel okay if I'm not willing.

ACCEPTANCE: TO NOTICE, TO KNOW, TO EMBRACE

When planning my family, I already had vivid dreams of our future. I imagined a curated set of milestones rolling out one by one, with cute mispronunciations, quirky hobbies, and gorgeous graduation photos. When Joey received a diagnosis of delays and a prescription for interventions, my dreams were delayed, and new plans of hard work appeared. I thought I could heal all his worsening symptoms myself. My to-do list expanded to include myriad therapies, food regimens, communication modalities, and mentoring a stream of babysitters. As the years went by with little forward momentum in his learning and skills, my original dreams slipped away altogether. My mission was to help him develop, then to temper his aggressive and self-injurious tantrums.

NOTICING JOEY

Acceptance can mean noticing or seeing something as it is. The opposite is being unaware. For years I watched time pass Joey by without affecting him, without magically growing him up. I realized how hard he was trying, and that all of the successes he managed were owed to him, not to my parenting prowess. This was quite a shift in my world view, as I had congratulated myself on the developmental trajectory of my first child.

Joey communicates with word approximations and his own rudimentary form of sign language to tell me about songs he likes and foods he wants. For years I wanted to know what he thought about so badly that I would occasionally dream that he could talk. I would wake up abuzz with our conversation. The reset to reality was flattening after the precious minutes of enjoying whatever unremarkable dialogue my brain had made up.

After years of a new step forward and another step back, I recognized that Joey's tentative progress in communication could be symbolized by an old-fashioned water wheel. Whenever he picked up a few new words, some others fell away.

I now know that Joey's aggressive and self-injurious behaviors are nearly all communication-based. During some of his tantrums I understood his point of view, but other times I had no idea what he wanted or protested. Experts repeatedly asked me if he was anxious, but I said no. Only after he moved away from our house, and his behaviors subsided, could I see the role anxiety played. Seeing anti-anxiety medication work for him further solidified the idea that Joey was experiencing anxiety. His expression of anxiety is different than I expected. The word "anxiety" had a broader meaning than I realized, and no one explained it to me. All the years that I said Joey didn't have anxiety, I wasn't noticing it. I was unaware.

KNOWING WHAT TO EXPECT FOR JOEY

Acceptance can mean knowing something. The opposite is denial. Knowing who Joey is in the moment is easy because he is an open book. Knowing what to expect for his future is both medically and emotionally difficult.

Looking at Joey as an infant with delays, I didn't know what to dream for his future. Which of all the possible trajectories would come true? If I only knew, I could have a chance at accepting it. When I rejoiced in a miniscule advance, I intentionally had blinders on to ignore the multitudes of things he still couldn't do. If I had known his diagnosis early in his life, it would've been terribly painful. The advantage would've been a prognosis, a target to try to reach or surpass.

As Joey aged without developing, I had no one to look to who had gone before us, no one who was on the same path as Joey. When I read about an adult with severe autism who one day started talking in full sentences and remembered his entire life experience, I found myself wondering whether I was holding on to a similar hope. When I noticed him lose words that he had been able to say the month before, and struggled with getting him appropriate nutrition, I wondered if I was catastrophizing the situation in despair. Even today, with a genetic diagnosis and futuristic treatments in development, I have no idea what to plan for, no idea what is realistic for Joey's future. Knowing what I don't know feels terribly heavy.

I think about how everyone has some uncertainty about life, but most people hold a mental picture of the future that can be shared. The loss of that vision, as happens with a severe diagnosis, is devastating. It shakes our understanding of the world and our place in it.

I can't see our future, but admitting that any vision of the future is an illusion lessens the blow.

EMBRACING JOEY, BUT MAYBY NOT EVERYTHING ELSE

Acceptance can mean embracing a reality, where the opposite is rejection. When I thought about acceptance around Joey's initial diagnosis of delays, I naively thought, "Of course I accept my son. I love him," as if rejection would not be part of my reality. But Joey's reality included many issues beyond his lingering babyhood and love of snuggling. I also needed to accept his first diagnosis, however incomplete, and the all-too-often conflicting diagnoses and recommendations from specialists. I needed to accept the change to our family's daily rhythms and long-term goals. I needed to accept that his prognosis was unknown and that finding caregivers able to help would be difficult and expensive. I needed to see the world clearly, see that it is not built for people like Joey, and understand which parts I might be able to change. I needed to embrace my altered role as a mother. None of these issues were easy for me to accept.

New issues continue to crop up for me to notice, examine, and embrace. For me, acceptance is a long journey that expands over time. I would like to share a few milestones on my path.

SO MANY POINTS OF ACCEPTANCE

When Joey was twelve months old, I helped him through his first diagnostic assessment prescribed by his pediatrician. He was several months behind in both the physical and cognitive domains. That sounded to me like a gap I could help him recover from, even though he was delayed by a third of his life. I accepted the work in front of us.

When Joey was three years old, I chanced upon something that shifted the way I thought about him. I saw a photo of a baby wearing a onesie that read: "I've stumped ten medical professionals today. What have you done?" I loved the message for its defiance, for taking the common ideal of esteemed intellectual prowess and flipping it to honor the one who was medically puzzling. It's the first time I remember feeling a little uppity, like when your child is on a winning team and no one dampens your celebration.

When he was four, Joey was diagnosed with autism, a complete turn-around from being told multiple times that he "definitely did not have autism." Joey had finally developed enough for us to observe some of the signs. The autism parent support groups I attended were full of great advice, but none of it was relevant to Joey's life. After a few painful months, I stopped going. I did not feel noticed or embraced in that community, or that I could be helpful to others.

I remember Joey's sixth birthday as the day I realized I needed to privately honor myself, in addition to his birthday celebration. I found a present to reward my diligent work that was not yet having an effect. I accepted that my life was altered forever. I let go of my career goals, and the goal of having a conversation with him. For months after that birthday, I perfected crying silently while chauffeuring my unsuspecting children.

The first day I accepted my identity as a special needs mom was a few years into attending a monthly lunch with six other moms.

They were grappling with a wide range of diagnoses and troubling behaviors from their children. They had all been supporting each other for years before I joined. They welcomed me right away. Their intentional kindness to each other and quick laughter wrapped me up in relief. Their kids were older than Joey and I received great advice and new perspectives. In talking to each other we recognized that our parenting situations often included extreme circumstances, so we called ourselves an extreme moms group rather than a special needs moms group.

When Joey was about nine years old, I finally felt comfortable enough to ask the extreme moms the question no one else could answer for me: "When will the sadness go away?" They blinked at each other for a moment before they all erupted in raucous laughter. The sadness, it seemed, was never going to go away. It might get less intense, but it was always present in some form. If just one of them had said this with a quiet sense of loss, I might have felt bereft. But the full force of their combined joy-through-pain showed me that I could accept the reality of living with lifelong sadness. It would not be the unbearable punishment I had imagined.

At age 16 we got the genetic diagnosis that explains all Joey's differences. I was shocked at its clear-cut certainty. I was surprised to find out just how relieved I was that his problems were not my fault. It feels shameful to even write that down. But finding out that he has a DNA variant was freeing in a way I had not expected. And reading about his disorder was both disappointing and liberating. Disappointing that the biology was a serious blow to his cognition and behavior, liberating because I now saw Joey for who he is: a rock star in the face of this debilitating lack of a particular protein in his brain.

More recently I reached a new level of acceptance about my identity as a special needs mom while reading a research paper about aging. The researchers sought a truly stressed-out group of people and showed they were aging faster than average. The group was mothers of children with special needs. *Oh shit!!* My initial shock was followed by profound grief. The grief helped me recognize that my constant body aches, excess weight, and diminished mental competence are actual health issues.

LOOKING BACK

I can't lie. I hate having to strive for acceptance. Before I have it, acceptance looks like giving in or giving up, it looks like not having high standards, it looks like defeat.
It is not.

Acceptance is the only way forward, with clear eyes and a full heart.

MY TAKEAWAYS

1. Acceptance gives me a solid place to start.

2. For me, acceptance means changing a thousand thoughts, from concrete specifics to my entire worldview.

3. My journey of accepting what it means to parent Joey has been long, surprising, and shows no signs of being over.

my frustrations are rooted in fear

I took advantage of all the programs designed to help Joey: medical, educational, and community, and nearly every one of them let me down or left me frustrated at some point. Even when people tried their best to help us, what Joey needed was typically out of the scope of what was offered.

During Joey's youth, our neighborhood preschool declined to handle him. Our friends with kids the same age were kind, but Joey's need for constant attention from me to keep him safe made our playdates pointless. I was holding onto the hope that he could catch up to his peers, so I put only cursory effort toward being a part of the special needs community. (Had we had our genetic diagnosis earlier I would have taken a different path. I would have been able to find people dealing with the same issues.) When I joined autism support groups or tried to connect with families from the birth-to-three center, we did not fit in as he was more severely affected or needed different accommodations than the other kids. I endured the lack of belonging in both the typical and atypical communities, the frustrations with conflicting advice from the experts, the lack of support from our schools. Each community let me down.

One of the first times that I was severely disappointed in the general public was on a plane with Joey when he was an infant. I cut short our family vacation in a foreign country because he had a fever, and I wanted to get him home where I could take better care of him. He was so sick that he was listless and silent, and I was worried. Person after person told me what a good baby he was. I clearly saw that people were saying "good babies" don't bother people. Why do so many people praise a baby for having none of the characteristics of vitality? In this case my fear blocked my ability to accept social niceties.

A few months after Joey's first birthday, we were ushered into the birth-to-three center, where the therapists were proud to include me in their planning. They asked me what he couldn't do, what I wanted for him. I listed all the things I worried about that he wouldn't do. I feel that most of these lovely, caring experts did not have a clue how to best help him or me. Most could not engage with my son. I learned to tell them about the few activities he enjoyed, with the one therapist he loved, so they could plan lessons that might work. Looking back, I wish they all had a better understanding of the minute steps in development so they could identify the next challenges that were useful to him. I wish they had not encouraged me to talk at length about what I wanted for him. My maternal instinct was to want him to be like his brothers. But the developmental trajectory of other people was always going to be irrelevant to Joey's journey.

As a newborn, Joey didn't look at things. At two months his vision hadn't seemed to improve. I started to wear striped shirts so his eyes would have something high-contrast and simple to focus on while I held him. Before he was six months old, I read about how complex it is to look at a human face, and how a face changes every fraction of a second. It can be overwhelming to people who don't filter information easily. I still don't know if this describes Joey, but I dearly wanted him to be able to look at my face. Throughout the day I sat in a chair with him and covered most of my face, wooing him to look and see just a little bit of me at a time. I would say the two things I felt were essential for him to know: "I'm your mom. I love you." Then I would reveal a different patch: an eye, or half my mouth. I'd repeat the same words. I simplified the tasks of looking at me and listening to my voice in hopes that it would help him. I don't remember anyone thinking this was a good use of my time. I could think of nothing more important. I was confident because I was not yet in real fear. My intuition was not blocked.

When Joey was two years old, I took him to an alternative specialist, a woman trained in Europe. She thought about brain development in the context of developing a dominant ear for hearing and a dominant hand, and she considered reflexes and patterns of movement. She mentioned in passing that he had "four-month-old vision," explaining that he didn't use his muscles to focus his eyes. I was shocked and outraged. The best-rated pediatric eye doctor in the city had just examined Joey at the birth-to-three clinic, where his vision was said to be fine. He could touch tiny things with his index finger, so I figured it was true. A trip to a developmental ophthalmologist (another specialty new to me) revealed that his eye exams were the same with and without dilation. He wasn't using his muscles to focus, which meant his brain wasn't directing the process.

Joey was prescribed glasses that corrected his distance vision by half, to get him to see a little better and help him to focus his eyes. Now that he was more physically capable than he was as an infant, it was quite difficult to get him accustomed to wearing glasses. I was frustrated with the original assessment, upset that I missed an obvious challenge in his development.

To say that Joey had a tough time in middle school would be a massive understatement. His teacher was very well respected, and she showed me her data indicating that all kids eventually learned to comply with the school day schedule. Joey told us over and over, with his self-injurious behaviors, that he could not or would not tolerate her school day plan. I didn't know of any other options and was advised by everyone – our pediatrician, family, other teachers – that staying the course would result in him learning to tolerate school. I was filled with fear. I was afraid of a future where he never learned to yield to the wishes of someone else. I was afraid of giving up my part-time job to school him myself. I mostly feared the increase in self-injury that I assumed would happen at home with me. His school had an experienced teacher and many skilled paraeducators, all trained and employed to help him.

Knowing what I know now about his genetic disorder, diagnosed when he was in high school, I try not to revisit decisions I made without all the relevant information. But the one regret I cannot shake is wishing I had pulled him out of middle school sooner. I do not know what alternate plan we would have come up with, but I now realize that advocating for him would have reduced his anxiety and overwhelm. I think the only thing he learned in that classroom was to reinforce his tendency to self-harm when upset. He was doing his best to tell me this was the wrong choice with his self-destructive behavior, and I wish I had found a way to honor that instead of listening to the "experts." But home schooling him would have been more of the same. What Joey needed was reduced anxiety. I didn't know that yet, and even if I had, I didn't know how to get it. I was making hundreds of small adjustments to our daily lives to try to help him, but he needed a bigger change. It took an overwhelming amount of self-injurious behavior from him in order for me to entertain the idea of him living apart from us. I held on to the status quo out of a lack of options and a debilitating fear.

LOOKING BACK

The gaps in care we have discovered and suffered through are incredibly frustrating. As Joey grew older, the lack of respite care and behavioral therapists became a tragedy for us. The lack of interdisciplinary medical specialists is truly mystifying. For example, to investigate Joey's eating issues, we have seen a nutritionist, gastrointestinal doctor, epileptologist, psychiatrist, behaviorist, and whoever oversaw the swallowing study. None gave us any actionable treatment options. Joey's issues with feeding, eating, swallowing, and being underweight should be seen as one large issue, addressed by an integrated team to solve his constellation of interrelated problems. When a doctor says, "This is not my area," for something adjacent to their specialty, I am especially unimpressed. It is not my area, either, yet here we are.

The intensity of my frustration is proportional to the amount of fear I feel. Some frustration is helpful for making change, to initiate action. But the excess, after the possible steps have been taken, can cause collateral damage to my well-being and my relationships.

MY TAKEAWAYS

1. The only expert in our situation is Joey. Observing him is the gold standard.

2. I built a team of experienced professionals. It is growing again now that he is an adult.

3. We are lucky to visit practitioners who care about Joey and work to ease some of his discomforts. None of them have yet improved Joey's developmental trajectory.

4. My best supporters ease my fears.

finding community
girlfriends and laughter are my relief

Despite being lucky enough to have caring and supportive people in my life, no one has experience in all the same issues I deal with while parenting Joey. When he was young with delays, he was an overly easy baby as long as I was holding him. I had two other small children, so I was exhausted from the sheer volume of physical care and lack of sleep. I didn't know yet how much support I was going to need. When he was diagnosed with autism at age four, I joined autism support groups but always left incredibly sad. Due to Joey's severe delays, we had none of the same struggles as the other families. When I met one mom at both the elementary school of my oldest child and also the specialized experimental preschool for Joey, my heart did cartwheels. But again, her journey was so different from mine that our friendship was based on us, not our kids – and I still had no support around Joey's many issues. It took time and lots of courage for me to find and foster the friendships I've made in my extreme moms lunch group. I joined their group despite my son being younger than their kids, and despite us all facing different primary issues. I knew I was struggling. I knew that when I was with them, I felt relief and could laugh again.

I am now grateful to be part of a club that I never wanted to be a member of. My friends in my extreme moms group help me navigate medical, educational, and behavioral challenges with their own expert advice, cautionary tales, and generous amounts of humor. We tell stories of ordinary life filled with grit, changing levels of hope, and details that we do not share widely. We recount how we make decisions for our children and how we try to assess the consequences. We comfort each other when talking about reducing our expectations. We cheer each other on when one has a victory, especially ones that most folks would not appreciate. When we gasp at behaviors, it is at those of unhelpful people, never the behaviors of our kids. We have each other's backs.

Talking with people who can handle the realities of my life, even if their daily experiences differ, has been incredibly important. Support comes from sharing without fear of offending, without fear of shame, and with the expectation of comfort and laughter. I am lucky: I made lifelong friends, and now have an emotional safety net. My long-term mental health is owed to these warriors, even while I see them less as the years go by.

Now that I know Joey's genetic diagnosis, I also rely heavily on friends online, parents of people with a pathogenic variant of the Syngap1 gene. My friends in our rare disease group are newer to me but just as precious. I learn from them and see echoes of Joey in so many of their kids.

Talking to others who understand the sacrifices, disappointments, and modifications in our lives is both special and essential. A sense of community arises from sharing the surprising joys and outrageous stories we live through; it has shored up my mental health and my sense of humor; it has reduced my fear.

Finding people in the world who are like Joey, and the families who love them, is an incredibly powerful gift.

LOOKING BACK

I have had help from precious friends and practitioners to know that even though Joey has issues that need to be fixed, his way of being in the world is valued and cherished, as is. They help me see that he is okay with himself. These thoughts tone down my fear.

Spending time with any friends who show their emotions and prioritize laughter and kindness is my primary strategy to get out of gravity and fear. Allowing others to see me takes courage. Calming myself helps my relationships and makes me a better parent.

MY TAKEAWAYS

1. Shifting my perspective to "Joey is okay" reduces my fear.

2. I try to let in small good things, especially when I'm missing the big things I want most.

3. My people are the people who have experience with similar situations, who can brainstorm creative solutions without pushing any particular option.

4. In order to feel support from others, I had to stop berating myself and stop holding myself to the impossible standard of curing Joey.

5. Letting a friend know what I'm going through is scary at first, but can lift my shame, dull my anger, pivot me away from disappointment, and connect me to another human.

6. Laughter is great medicine for my disappointment, fear, anger, and shame.

feel better now

I want to feel like a great parent. When I was focused on Joey's development, I was following one of my most strongly held values. But nothing improved his prognosis. By concentrating on our relationship, I found more success. It's important to note that Joey's development isn't less important to me. I will always want to heal him and grow up his brain. But my daily goals turned toward strengthening our bond in the midst of overwhelming grief, exhaustion, guilt, anger, disappointment, and shame. That's a journey that required time and intensive self-reflection. I had to contend with the thoughts and emotions holding me back from my innate pride and joy, preventing me from feeling like myself.

WHAT CAN I CONTROL?

Word choice is one of the few parts of our struggle over which I have control. The words I use to navigate our life reflect my level of acceptance. The way I speak about our situation changes depending on who's listening. When it's a loved one who feels bad about not being able to help me, I'm likely to downplay my struggles. When telling a doctor or therapist about us, I'll balance a challenge that needs attention with a strength. When I talk to Joey, I use positive or neutral language. But when I'm alone with my thoughts, I can be surprisingly negative. It turns out that I'm great at being very hard on myself, something I wouldn't do in front of others. Recognizing the ramifications of my words made a huge difference to me. My discoveries were so worthwhile, I want to share them here in two more vignettes.

The questions we ask: age 6

how are we the same?

After Joey's sixth birthday, I am devastated inside. He's still not talking. There's been no meaningful progress for years. Part of me has already let go of the hope that his stagnant 18-month-old abilities will start catching up with those of his peers, which feels disloyal of me. Begrudgingly, I let go of the rest. Now that I'm released from that unhelpful holding pattern, I am free to paint myself a bleak picture of his future. I create a mental list of things Joey will never do himself, based on my own daily actions.

He won't change lanes on the freeway.
He won't make doctor appointments.
He won't plan a party.
He won't care for others.

Every thought makes me sad, and I'm ashamed for dwelling on them.

I stay in my grief for a while. I don't share these thoughts with others, as I'm embarrassed to be grieving something that's been obvious for so long. I finally get fed up with my sorry self, endlessly listing numerous ways we're different, and ask a better question:

"How are we the same?"

I don't even have a realistic guess.

But I reason that there must be some non-trivial ways that we're similar. So I think about how I can find them.

I consider what activities Joey likes and wonder why. I know he loves going to the gymnastics center every week with his classroom. They say he especially likes the balance beam. I start looking for things for him to walk on when we're together: a log, a curb, a painted line on the pavement. I lead him to each mock balance beam, tap it with my shoe, and say "Up." He holds my hand and walks on the narrow linear path. To my surprise, he participates in this activity at every opportunity. By watching him, I realized that his level of engagement is interested but not intense, and his level of competence is ok but not perfect. He's having fun with a small challenge. I think about my own activities and how I like throwing a neighborhood tea party -- something creative and beautiful that isn't daunting. I remember how struggling to learn to play bridge was grueling, and how I'm glad I stopped. I realize we both appreciate frequent opportunities for appropriate challenges. They are simple ways to feel happiness right now, not ways to improve.

I think about when Joey looks the most relaxed and at peace. I see it whenever we're outside in the woods. He walks among the quiet, immobile trees, shaded from bright sun, or sits in the soft dirt and fallen leaves. He is satisfied and engaged. When he is in a pool, bouncy and grinning, he pushes the water, splashing. Like everyone else, he relishes sensory joy. His neurological differences make some common environments uncomfortable for him. Joey squints under the bright overhead lights in his school gym, but he can't indicate his pain or irritation, and so he throws a tantrum. He insists on turning a ball cap so that the brim doesn't shade his eyes. Once I supply his teacher with a bucket hat for him to wear during indoor PE, Joey's aggressive and self-injurious behaviors in the gym vanish. He can enjoy his favorite subject at school.

Watching Joey enjoy his time in the forest or a pool has prompted me to spend more time doing things I enjoy that aren't necessarily productive, like arranging fabrics or yarns from my stash just to see how the colors and textures look together. Knowing about Joey's sensitivities makes me more accepting of my own. I'm more prepared with hats and sunglasses, more willing to reduce my time in environments that feel harsh to me, even when others expect me to join in their fun. For a good life, we both need our senses to feel good (at least some of the time) and to limit feeling poorly. We need sensory joy.

We both love to be adored. In addition to his immediate and large extended family, Joey interacts with many different caregivers, teachers, and therapists who delight in him. He accepts hugs and he connects with people who share his sense of humor and his enjoyment of song mashups. I have always felt driven to develop and maintain close personal relationships, and I love being understood and appreciated. That we share this need is the least surprising to me – but I need help to figure out how best to foster a close relationship with Joey where we can both enjoy each other and feel adored more of the time.

I am relieved to have identified meaningful ways we're similar. It helps explain our best times together. I use the information to guide our daily interactions, and strive to include all three: appropriate challenges, sensory joy, and authentic adoration.

LOOKING BACK

Knowing how to simultaneously accept and work on Joey's development evolved as I learned more about Joey, myself, and the world. I have worked with him on communication, cognitive tasks, emotional regulation, daily routines, physical development, fine motor development, sensory play, and so much more. The shift to working on our relationship does not mean I don't care about helping his development. It just means that I have relaxed my constant search for improvements. I still notice and celebrate these when they happen. I just don't feel defeated every moment that they don't happen, which is most of the time. By concentrating on how we're similar, I find it more fun to plan our time together and I find it less exhausting to spend time together. I try to make sure we both have appropriate challenges, sensory joy, and authentic adoration.

MY TAKEAWAYS

1. I can control what I ask myself, what my goals are, and how I tell my story.

2. Thinking about what Joey loves and why he loves it proves to be a good use of my time.

3. Shifting my focus from how I can help him to how we can have a good time together might sound indulgent, but I think it's actually great parenting.

4. My main goal as the mom of all three of my children is to help them know that they are awesome.

5. When we are aligned and happy, having a positive experience together, Joey feels it. Saying "you're so great and I'm proud of you," doesn't communicate that to him, especially if I'm tired, sad, frustrated, or scared.

Corollary thoughts: age 11

a sleep-deprived mom walks into a coach

For several difficult years of sleep deprivation for me and escalating behaviors for Joey, I'm stuck in an ironclad story of factual woe. "Catching up" with friends includes me producing a list of grievances, describing issues beyond the realm of typical parenting. No one thinks or dares to challenge my incontrovertibly sad facts. The problem is that the story amplifies my devastation. Then one day, when Joey is eleven years old, I meet a woman who helps me get unstuck. While reading her blog, I'm attracted to her brand of sassy honesty and her humorous-plus-sarcastic take on mothering. (Find her at www.lineleoff.com). Without knowing what I'm getting into, I enroll in her class. In her life coaching group, Lin gets to know me and eventually, gently, lovingly, asks me to say one true thing about Joey. "He has a hard time communicating." I have firsthand knowledge of this fact and multiple experts have all put it in writing.

Lin helps me uncover the unstated, nearly invisible corollary thoughts that follow my initial statement every time – the thoughts that leave me forlorn.

I must help him learn to speak.

No one else can.

I don't know how.

Every time I say, "He has a hard time communicating," the shorthand in my brain rushes straight through those three sentences to the weight of letting him down. No wonder I am so sad. When others say the same fact, they don't follow up with the same sense of responsibility and helplessness.

The fix, she says, is to set those words aside and to think something else, something that is also true and feels a lot better.

I can't think of a thing.

Lin challenges me again: "He doesn't seem to have a hard time communicating at all. Do you ever not understand how he's feeling?" Of course I can tell when he's calm or upset, he's an open book. "What about, 'He is authentic.' Is that true?" she prompts.

I laugh and tear up. I think about my conversation with Adam about how he will learn to hide himself from me. Joey doesn't ever hide intent or reaction. I don't think he could be anything other than authentic, and I suspect he wouldn't want to. "He is authentic" becomes my new mantra. It connects me to my pride and delight. It bypasses my descent into guilt. It's the most powerful thing I didn't know I needed – the power to examine my thoughts and choose those that support me rather than drain me.

LOOKING BACK

Building relationships is always work, but building one with Joey took more. It took help from others. It took time alone for reflection. It took learning how to treat myself with grace.

MY TAKEAWAYS

1. True thoughts can be draining or lifting.

2. Small shifts can make a world of difference.

PARENT COACHING

T he changes I've described in this book were hard-won. I was so sure that I was living in alignment with my priorities that I could not conceive of a change inside me that would improve my life. Getting unstuck felt noteworthy, transformational, liberating, and deeply personal.

I was so excited by the positive changes in my inner world that I sought out the best parent coaching training program. I found it at The Parent Coaching Institute® (PCI, thepci.org), and I am proud to now be a PCI-Certified Parent Coach®. PCI built its program on theories of organizational development and the model of executive coaching. An executive coach helps executives understand their own priorities and values, as well as those of their company, employees, and clients. They help people be the best executives they can be. However, an executive coach does not make business decisions! Similarly, a parent coach supports clients in being the best parents they can be without making any parenting decisions.

The full scope of parent coaching is vast. It can cover parent-child relationships, work and school issues, household daily rhythms, child activities and friendships, or anything else that a client wants to improve. There are no limits. The client comes with a willingness to have conversations and a desire for a change. The parent coach listens deeply and is curious about the client's experience, without judgement. The parent coach reflects the client's words and asks questions to clarify their views. Clients might feel exhilarated or relieved. Sometimes it's uncomfortable because growth is sometimes uncomfortable. Parent coaching isn't a substitute for counseling, and it isn't about transferring specific expert information. Parent coaching grows the client's capacity to grow, which improves both their parenting and other aspects of their life.

Parent coaching is comprised of conversations that help people envision a better future and make it a reality. I am delighted to be able to provide coaching conversations for parents like myself – people who are trying hard and just want to feel good about their parenting. Over the phone or on video calls, we discuss their challenges, strengths, and what they want more of in their lives. Then we design small trials of action items to find what helps. Sometimes a change in the client's behavior changes their child's behavior. Sometimes noticing something new leads to a perspective shift. Clients find more energy, notice friction decrease, see developmental leaps, and bridge gaps in their relationships. Coaching isn't ongoing. To generate sustainable change, it typically lasts eight to twelve sessions, either weekly or every two weeks. Before accepting new clients, I ask for a 30-minute phone call to learn if coaching with me is a good fit. There are many effective coaches out there and feeling seen and heard by your coach is essential.

LOOKING AHEAD

My experiences parenting Joey and his neurotypical brothers feel important and universal. My quest for clarity helps my clients identify the specific changes they want. My intuition leads to novel insights. My creativity and unusual perspective inspire surprising suggestions.

In my coaching conversations, I feel more like myself than I have in a long time. I am energized by listening deeply to people who are striving for improvement. I feel joy when I help people have more ease and peace in their family life, or help them have pride in their parenting. I know this is the right path for me.

Do you want to understand yourself better as a parent? Do you want to strengthen your connection with your child? You can start the process right now. No matter where you are on your journey, it is always the right time to feel like a great parent.

NEXT STEPS

1. To see if coaching conversations with me are right for you, use the contact form at JanieReade.com

2. Or find another great coach at thePCI.org

I had no idea

J oey has taught me things that I had no idea I didn't know. With-out him, I would define success more narrowly: by external validation rather than internal change. Without him, I would not understand the role of physical and emotional development in cogni-tion. Without him, I would probably be satisfied to use my brain the way I was trained instead of striving to alter my thought processes. I wouldn't understand my own dislikes in relation to my sensory profile. I wouldn't recognize that I arrange flowers and sew quilts for their visual beauty. I would not have felt the urgency to write down my thoughts in an attempt to clarify them.

Without Joey, I would not understand that the acceptance of one person's limits can lead to the ability to show grace to anyone.

Big hugs to you from someone who may recognize parts of the path you travel.

XO - JR

GET IN TOUCH

Which parts of my story feel the same for you, and what is different?
What do you most want to improve for yourself and your family?

I'd love to hear from you. Email me at connect@janiereade.com

ABOUT THE AUTHOR

Janie Reade is a pen name I use to keep the identity of my family, including that of my vulnerable child, private. I don't know what the future holds for Joey's awareness around who he is and whether he will resent being written about. I know that he doesn't like me talking about him with other adults, at least not in front of him.

I've learned about parenting and about life from an amazing group of teachers, therapists, friends, and my own incredible family. I am on a journey I didn't ask for, but once presented with it, I chose it with my whole heart and mind. Ever since I was a child, I wanted to be the best mother I could be. I had a great example in my mom, who gave me a strong philosophy and excellent training when taking care of my younger siblings and as the neighborhood babysitter.

I was a scientist before becoming a mother, and I've either been a stay-at-home mom or worked part time since having three boys in under four years. I have now retired from a science career for good.

I'm part of the Syngap Research Fund community of volunteers. Learn and donate at syngapresearchfund.org I help parents understand genetic reports for their children with neurodevelopmental disorders. I participate in basic science in meetings with academic and industry scientists to accelerate the research and development of treatments for Syngap1 disorders.

I am a parent coach. I earned certification in 2022 from the Parent Coach Certification Training Program at The Parent Coach Institute. Learn more at thepci.org. The PCI has been training coaches around the world since 2001.

I live in the United States. My languages are English and Joey Sign Language.

ACKNOWLEDGEMENTS

This book was inspired by a master coach, Lin Eleoff. I have been helped by many friends and family who read drafts and gave essential feedback. Early concepts were guided by C.L. and J.A. Later drafts were read by B.S., A.R., H.R., A.E., J.K., and many others. I'm grateful to you all. Thanks to K.M. for so many edits that sound more like me. Thank you to Marni Seneker, book coach, whose encouragement gave me the confidence to publish.

Thank you to Gloria DeGaetano for the Foreword -- it is thrilling to have this physical manifestation of nurturing attention from my teacher and mentor. I believe she is the reason parent coaching exists as a structured discipline. I want to thank my early editor Ann Deiterich and initial cover artist Rhianon Paige. A huge thank you to Gyoung Soon Choi, my friend who donated her time to design and format the eBook and paperback print book.

Thank you to all the wonderful parents and volunteers who make up the Syngap Research Fund. You have all made me feel welcome, appreciated, and valued. I love getting to know you all as we work for relevant treatments for our precious people. Whether you have a youngster or an adult, our lives overlap. I hope this book helps to foster connection in our community. And to readers dealing with other diagnoses, or any issues that feel complex or overwhelming, I hope you find something that resonates with you within these pages.

I am grateful to the following people, who honor Joey in so many ways. Thank you to M.D., for listening and celebrating us. I am indebted to C.A., for visiting with Joey and for introducing me to parent coaching. I'm lucky to have a long and dear friendship with V.N. who gives me great perspective, fine details, and tangible and intangible encouragements. She is a true thought partner. I want to thank K.M., C.S., K.P., S.P., and all the lunch group moms for their glorious leadership in my life. I must thank my brother M. who devoted so many days off to spend time with Joey. His intentional relationship-building shows me how I want to be.

Thank you to my mother and sister who give me rest when I am too tired, and laughter when I am too serious. I want to thank my husband and neurotypical sons who cheer me on every time I have a mission, including writing this book. Your input was invaluable.

Finally, I'm grateful to Joey. He has taught me so much already and continues to help me learn.

Printed in Great Britain
by Amazon

16707747R00058